# The Solitude of Loneliness

# The Solitude of Loneliness

by
JOHN C. WOODWARD

with
Janel Queen

Lexington Books

*D.C. Heath and Company / Lexington, Massachusetts / Toronto*

*Library of Congress Cataloging-in-Publication Data*

Woodward, John C., 1924–
The solitude of loneliness.

Includes index.
1. Loneliness. 2. Solitude. I. Queen, Janel.
II. Title.
BF575.L7W66 1988 158'.2 86-45864
ISBN 0-669-14504-1 (alk. paper)
ISBN 0-669-14505-X (pbk. : alk. paper)



Published simultaneously in Canada
Printed in the United States of America
Casebound International Standard Book Number: 0-669-14504-1
Paperbound International Standard Book Number: 0-669-14505-X
Library of Congress Catalog Card Number: 86-45864

The paper used in this publication meets the minimum requirements of American National Standard for Information Sciences—Permanence of Paper for Printed Library Materials, ANSI Z39.48-1984.

ISBN 0-669-14504-1

88 89 90 91 92 8 7 6 5 4 3 2 1

*To*

TRUDY

*Whose loss caused intense loneliness*

*and*

HARRIETTE, EMILY, JOHN, JR., AMY, MATT AND OSCAR

*Whose love diminishes it*

# Contents

# Preface

OVER twenty years ago, a significant experience not only changed my life but put me on a path that culminated in this book. I was living in Coral Gables, Florida, with my family: Trudy, my wife; Emily, our daughter, who was twelve years old; and our son, John, Jr., who was eight. I was on leave from San Jose State College in California working at the University of Miami as director of research for a project designed to improve teaching in higher education.

Eight and a half years earlier, while I was in the process of finishing my Ph.D. degree at the University of Nebraska, Trudy had been hospitalized with congestive heart failure, caused by a heart problem that resulted from childhood rheumatic fever. The emergency was compounded by the fact that she was three months pregnant with John, Jr. The choice the physicians gave her was to have an abortion or heart surgery. Abortions were illegal at that time except to save the life of the mother, and heart surgery was very new and crude by today's standards. Despite the risks, Trudy chose the surgery; John, Jr., was born six months later.

We had been living in Miami only one and a half years when she started having heart problems again. She had read somewhere that impacted wisdom teeth could cause the kind of heart trouble she was experiencing, and she became obsessed with the idea that her impacted wisdom teeth were contributing to her heart problem. She convinced her physicians that she needed to have her wisdom teeth extracted. Because of her heart condition, she was admitted to the hospital to have them removed. Her heart was too weak to take the procedure, and she died.

We had been married over fifteen years and had what I, and I think Trudy, considered a good, happy marriage. Now she was suddenly gone, and I was left alone with our two children, far from relatives and close friends. We had made many friends in Miami, and they were most supportive in this time of crisis, but they were not the same as long-time friends and family.

I was devastated. I had suffered losses before, but compared to this one, they were nothing. I remember experiencing the unbearable pain of grief and loneliness. I felt cut off and isolated from someone who had been close to me for so long. I wanted desperately to talk to her, to tell her about each day's events, to ask her advice, to be near her. But she was gone.

Emily had been emotionally close to her mother and was at an important developmental stage when Trudy died. She was at that point in life when daughters need a mother to talk with. John, Jr., had also been very attached to his mother and, like most other eight-year-old boys, dependent on her for so much. They too were devastated. As I talked with them in the early morning the day their mother died, I remember telling them that they were too young to have to endure this kind of pain.

I began to search for ways to help me and my children deal with our grief and loneliness. This search set me on a quest that has never ended. As any good college professor would do, I began to search the literature for information and help. I found that philosophers talked about grief and loneliness, poets wrote poems about it, and there were thousands of songs, but there was almost no research on the subject. The professional literature had paid little attention to loneliness. The various social sciences had all but ignored the subject.

When I returned to the University of Nebraska, I remembered something one of my college professors had told me years before: "If you really want to make a contribution to the profession and cut out a 'niche' for yourself, do your research on a topic of great interest but where very little has been done." Loneliness seemed like a perfect topic. It would serve a dual purpose: help me and my children understand and cope with our loneliness and provide that niche.

For over twenty years, I have been researching loneliness and solitude with my students and publishing the results, for the most part in professional research journals. Now I am ready to share and discuss the research findings with others to enable them to understand and cope with loneliness and solitude.

My children and I made the adjustment. Although we went through some difficult times emotionally, we had to adjust. About a year after Trudy's death, I accepted a position at the University to Nebraska so that we could be close to family. I married again, and Harriette and I had two children, Amy and Matt. Amy is a student at Texas Christian University and Matt a high school senior. John, Jr., and Emily are married and have completed master's degrees. John and his wife, Sandy, have given us our first grandchild, Trudy.

Life goes on and loneliness, for the most part, is blotted out.

# Acknowledgments

THIS book is based primarily on the research accomplished by students and faculty in the Department of Human Development and the Family at the University of Nebraska–Lincoln over the past twenty years. Material was taken from research projects completed by: M.L. Bauermeister, J.T. Donlan, D.A. Gladbach, K.L. Hornung, J.B. Joern, V. Kalyan-Masih, P.M. Luck, N.P. Medora, B.W. Otto, S.K. Seevers, C.K. Swanson, C.A. Travis, M.J. Visser, H. Woodward, J.C. Woodward, M. Wythers, and J.R. Zabel. Acknowledgments also go to the Agricultural Research Division, Institute of Agriculture and Natural Resources, University of Nebraska–Lincoln, for initial and continuing support of this research.

# The Solitude of Loneliness

# 1

# What Is Loneliness?

LONELINESS is solitary. It is something we do by ourselves; no one can do it for us or with us. Nor is it something we can share, for when we begin to share it, it disappears. The prescription for life and the antidote for loneliness is human interaction.

This book is about loneliness and how it affects each of us throughout our lives. Loneliness is a subject familiar to everyone and probably one of the most important dimensions of human existence. All of us experience loneliness in varying degrees at some time or another—some a great deal more than others. Philosopher Erich Fromm said, "Like the common cold, loneliness is easy to catch, hard to cure, rarely fatal but always unpleasant and sometimes wretched almost beyond bearing." When evangelist Billy Graham was asked which problem plagued more people than any other, he answered with a single word: "loneliness." Paul Tournier, a Swiss psychiatrist, believes that loneliness is the most devastating malady of our age.

People who say that they are never lonely are probably kidding themselves or do not fully understand the concept. Loneliness is a fact of life; we all must contend with it. If we do not cope with it, we die from it. Loneliness is always present to a degree; there is no complete escape. Indeed it is part of living, of being human, of loving and being loved, of caring and being cared for. It can be a devastating experience—or a creative one.

From the moment of separation at birth to the end of life, we are on our own. Everyone wants and needs to be their own person, but being completely independent of others may be an extremely lonely experience.

Psychologist Clark Moustakas has observed that "to love is to be lonely." He adds, "All love leads to suffering. If we did not care for others in a deep and fundamental way, we would not experience grief when they are troubled or disturbed, when they face tragedy or misfortune, when they are ill and dying." The price of love is loneliness. Moustakas has also written, "In the absence of the loved one, in solitude and loneliness, a new self emerges, in solitary thought."

Preschool children want desperately to "do it myself" and to experience new things, but they may cry bitterly from separation anxiety and loneliness when they are left at nursery school or at home with a sitter. The first day of kindergarten may be a day of tears and unhappiness, but the end of the day brings joy at the sight of the parent and the sharing of the day's accomplishments. Young adolescents strive to be different but at the same time want to be accepted by their peers. In order to gain this acceptance, they must be like their peers. They want to be individual and autonomous but at the same time to be identified as part of the group. This is the paradox of our desire for relationships and group identification while preserving our individuality. Teenagers rejoice in their emancipation, independence, and individualism, but this new independence is often accompanied by deep feelings of loneliness.

The adolescent off to college with a sense of new-found freedom and independence may also suffer intense feelings of homesickness, grief, depression, and loneliness. After the initial adjustment, however, this same adolescent probably can't wait to get back to campus after spring or summer break.

For many adolescents, college is their first time away from friends and family for any length of time. Many are torn between adjusting to a new situation in a place far from home and wishing they could retain the same level of interaction with friends from high school. One college freshman attending a university 650 miles from her home felt guilty when she was having a good time with her new friends. She said, "I hate what is happening to me. I am having a wonderful time, but I was so close to all my friends at home, and I don't want to lose that closeness." Although she was making a natural adjustment to her new situation, she felt guilty about it.

Parents of children undergoing these changes—to nursery-school, to kindergarten, to college—also may feel, as their children do, a sense of loss and grief that leads to feelings of loneliness. But time and a chance to adjust to these changes brings pride and satisfaction at the accomplishments of their children.

These losses are all in the category of essential losses; they are necessary for human development. But although we know that these losses must be endured for development to proceed in a natural and positive way, this knowledge doesn't make the grief any easier.

## Meanings of Loneliness

When asked, "What is loneliness?" a small four-year-old boy answered, "When you talk to yourself and nobody doesn't love you." His five-year-old sister replied, "It's when you are all alone, and your mommy and daddy are mad at you." These definitions are pretty good considering the age of the children.

Researchers at the University of Nebraska have been conducting a scientific investigation of loneliness and solitude for over twenty years. They are trying to find better definitions of loneliness, to determine how often and with what intensity it occurs, when and under what circumstances it is present throughout the life cycle, and the relationship of loneliness to other aspects of life.

The concept of loneliness is difficult to define because it has so many special meanings to most people. It has been defined as "the condition of an individual who desires contact with others but is unable to achieve it," "A basic sense of unconnectedness with people," "Absence of love," "A lack or loss of friendship," "A feeling of not being meaningfully related."

Some of the definitions for loneliness given by research subjects in the studies were: "No friends, no happiness, no laughter, no smiles," "Never hearing from loved ones, either by letter or phone calls," "Being without purpose," "Without love," "Not having anyone to share the bad times and the good times together," and "A feeling that no one cares or would miss me if I wasn't here."

Some children said: "Not having anyone to share with or talk to," "Being without friends," "People putting you down because you do something different," "A bad relationship with your family," "There is no one to share your joy or sorrow," "Nobody loves me," "Growing up," and "Not having someone who cares."

Although loneliness is universal, it clearly has no universal definition. It is a concept that everyone must define individually. Loneliness is personal. Loneliness is subjective. Loneliness is inside us. Loneliness is existential. Loneliness is situational. Loneliness is transient. Loneliness is destructive. Loneliness is creative. Loneliness is persistent. Loneliness is all these things and more.

The philosophical or subjective definition used for the purposes of the Nebraska loneliness studies was: "A feeling of being alone and disconnected or alienated from positive persons, places, or things."

Loneliness is not to be confused with solitude. Synonyms for solitude include exile, isolation, leisure, quarantine, relaxation, retirement, detachment, isolation, privacy, quiet, and seclusion.

## Meanings of Solitude

There is much confusion concerning the terms *loneliness* and *solitude*. A recent newspaper account about Dorothy Molter, who died at the age of seventy-nine, related that Molter was the last permanent resident of a remote million-acre wilderness area in northern Minnesota. She had lived there alone in her log cabin for fifty-six years. In 1952 the *Saturday Evening Post* called her "The Loneliest Woman in America." But Molter said, "I've never been lonely in my life." The *Saturday Evening Post* had equated solitude with loneliness.

Loneliness and solitude may occur together, but one does not necessarily follow the other. Solitude is aloneness, being physically alone. It is something we may choose for ourselves. All of us spend some time alone each day. This time alone does not always lead to loneliness; we may enjoy being alone at times, and therefore are not lonely. Many highly creative people—authors, poets, scientists, inventors, artists, and others—seek uninterrupted solitude in order to be creative. Solitude is concerned with our outside world; loneliness comes from our inside world. You may be surrounded by people and be lonely or be all alone in a desert and not be lonely at all.

Solitude may enable us to refresh ourselves, to rest, to gather our thoughts, to think things through. It can be a period when we have the time and the inclination to evaluate relationships with friends and loved ones. Going away to college, sickness, death, travel, moves, transfers, and other separations may force us to consider many things we have taken for granted. We may be physically alone but feel the presence of friends, family, and other support networks that are an important part of our lives.

Solitude may not always be something we choose. When it is not, we may suffer untold loneliness. Social outcasts; skid row alcoholics, drinking wine from bottles in paper sacks; drug addicts staring at the wall of a building; the homeless and friendless, wandering about at night or sleeping in bus stations; bag ladies who walk the streets of cities; AIDS victims; and the abandoned elderly living all alone: these people are just some of the casualties of forced solitude who may be pathetically lonely.

If you are now curious about your own loneliness, take the Loneliness Inventory (Short Form) presented here and then compare your loneliness score with the following average scores obtained by individuals in other groups:

## LONELINESS INVENTORY

Directions: Respond as honestly as you can to each of the following items in the light of your typical attitude over a period of time.

| *I Am Lonely . . .* | *Almost Always* | *Often* | *Some-times* | *Rarely* | *Nev* |
|---|---|---|---|---|---|
| 1. When I am alone | 4 | 3 | 2 | 1 | 0 |
| 2. When I am without transportation for a long period of time | 4 | 3 | 2 | 1 | 0 |
| 3. When finances are not available to participate in activities | 4 | 3 | 2 | 1 | 0 |
| 4. When I don't feel appreciated by others | 4 | 3 | 2 | 1 | 0 |
| 5. When I can't seem to develop friendships | 4 | 3 | 2 | 1 | 0 |
| 6. When I feel left out or rejected by others | 4 | 3 | 2 | 1 | 0 |
| 7. When I am thinking about the past | 4 | 3 | 2 | 1 | 0 |
| 8. When I can't do things with others | 4 | 3 | 2 | 1 | 0 |
| 9. On my birthday | 4 | 3 | 2 | 1 | 0 |
| 10. When I think about my family | 4 | 3 | 2 | 1 | 0 |

The following directions will give you the necessary information to score your Loneliness Inventory.

## SCORING

Add number of "Almost Always" responses ____ × 4 = ____
Add number of "Often" responses ____ × 3 = ____
Add number of "Sometimes" responses ____ × 2 = ____
Add number of "Rarely" responses ____ × 1 = ____
Add number of "Never" responses ____ × 0 = __0__
LONELINESS SCORE TOTAL = ____divided by 10 = ____

## YOUR RESPONSES

The higher is your score, the lonelier you are.
A score of 4 means you are almost always lonely.

A score of 3 means you are often lonely.
A score of 2 means you are sometimes lonely.
A score of 1 or 0 means that you are rarely or never lonely or that perhaps you were not completely honest with yourself in responding to the statements. If that is the case, go back and look at the test again.

| *Comparison Group from Research Studies* | *Average Loneliness Score* |
|---|---|
| Senior high school girls (urban) | 2.99 |
| Rural adolescents | 2.74 |
| Rural adults | 2.36 |
| Freshmen and senior girls in rural high schools | 2.11 |
| Low-income single adolescent mothers | 2.06 |
| Alcoholic subjects | 1.93 |
| Freshmen college students | 1.90 |
| Low-income single-parent mothers | 1.89 |
| Freshmen and seniors in rural high schools | 1.89 |
| Divorced adults | 1.59 |
| Never-married young adults | 1.26 |
| Housewives | 1.21 |
| Older urban widows | 1.03 |
| Elderly in homes for the elderly | .83 |
| Elderly | .78 |

If your loneliness score is higher than you would like it to be, worrying will only make you lonelier. In the chapters that follow, you will gain a better understanding of loneliness and perhaps learn how to cope with it. If you have a low loneliness score, congratulations. By reading this book, you may find out how you can help others in their loneliness. (The Long Form of the Loneliness Inventory appears in the Appendix.)

Loneliness and how it relates to individual development through several important stages in the life cycle—childhood, adolescence, the middle years, and the later years—will be discussed. This information will be tied together by relating the common factors that always seem to be associated with loneliness. Finally, we will look at ways to cope with loneliness.

# 2

# Childhood

LONELINESS in childhood is a much neglected and little understood area. Most think of childhood as a time of fun and games. They think that because we live in a child-centered society and are alert and responsive to the needs of children, children couldn't possibly be lonely. The truth of the matter is that childhood is far from being totally happy for a large segment of society, and we are not child centered. Although we may be somewhat more alert and responsive than in the past, children today do experience loneliness.

Children experience loneliness for many reasons. One of the major causes is separation from parents or primary care givers. Over half the mothers of school-age children and 33 percent of preschool children work outside the home; thus, many children come home to an empty house after school, and the preschool child spends the day separated from parents.

An estimated 1.4 million children in the nation each year are victims of abuse and neglect. Reported cases of child abuse have increased 80 percent in the last ten years. Abused and neglected children experience extreme helplessness and loneliness.

Divorce also affects large numbers of children. Over one million couples divorce each year, and 70 percent have children. Half of the children born today will live at least temporarily with only one parent. Many suffer shock at the idea of separation from a parent and feel guilty because they are afraid that they may have caused the problem between their parents. They also feel rejection from the parent who moves apart from the family.

Countless children suffer in silence in what may be an oppressive school situation. Often, adults won't listen to their complaints simply because they are children. They feel helpless and lonely.

Children are sometimes very cruel to other children who are not physically attractive, athletic, smart, or who are not able to dress in the best clothes. These children may feel isolated and lonely.

## Infancy

After nine months of warm closeness in the womb of the mother, the newborn is suddenly expelled, separated from mother, whisked off to the bright lights of the hospital nursery, and placed in an "isolate." Just at the time when the baby needs a mother, she is not there. The nurses who efficiently go about their duties of attending to the needs of several infants are not the same as cuddling close to "mommy." Some psychologists have built a whole counseling theory around the trauma that occurs with this separation at birth.

Some hospitals do have birthing rooms where the infant is not taken away from the mother and hurried off to the nursery but left to be cuddled and loved and assured. The father and siblings may also be included. In most hospitals, however, standard medical practice is to separate the infant from the mother and bring the infant back only for scheduled visits and feeding. Even then the mother may have to wear a mask to protect the child from germs, and the father is seldom included. Siblings are not even allowed to see their mother until she comes home.

A few days later, the infant is taken home where "ideally" a nursery awaits, complete with a crib, situated as far away from the rest of the family living space as possible so he or she won't be disturbed by other members of the family. To top it off, just after the infant has gotten used to the bright lights of the hospital nursery and the somewhat frantic activity of that environment, we turn off all the lights and close the door of the nursery to keep it quiet.

New parents often hear that they have to learn not to "spoil" the child by going into his or her room in response to every cry. They are told: "If you have just changed her, that can't be the problem, and she can't be hungry because it is not time for the next feeding," "All he wants is some attention; you can't let him get away with that. He could learn to expect it, and then you are in for a lot of trouble." Perhaps these examples are overdrawn a little to make a point, and they are not true in all cases; but they are close enough to the truth that many parents will recognize them.

## Hospital Experience

Children who must be hospitalized often find the experience difficult. In one case, a ten-month-old child with a severe respiratory flu required hospitalization. Since she was "contagious," the parents were told that she had to be isolated, even from them. The parents, young and inexperienced, allowed this separation and watched helplessly through a glass window while doctors put the necessary tubes in the baby's head and legs to correct the dehydration. The baby screamed all this time—perhaps from pain but surely also from the fear of suddenly finding herself cut off from her significant others at a time when she needed them. The parents continued their vigil through the glass for three long days. The nurses tried to help, but the child never seemed to stop crying.

The psychological trauma this child suffered in the separation from her parents during this period of extreme stress for her left scars that persisted. When the parents got her home, she clung to them; she would not let them put her down even when she fell asleep in their arms. When they put her on their bed, they had to lie down beside her and hold her close before she would go to sleep. She had to be touching them. It was two weeks before these parents could get her back into her own bed.

Stranger anxiety and separation anxiety start when children are about eight months old. The child who has been happy as long as someone, not necessarily a parent, is around suddenly becomes frightened of strangers and has problems with being left by the familiar care giver. Later, a bad hospital experience may cause prolonged problems that can turn into great fear of strangers and separation anxiety at day care and school. Therefore the stress associated with the necessary hospital experience should be lowered as much as possible for the child.

Clark Moustakas reports in his book *Loneliness* that he had experienced loneliness many times, but it was not until a hospital experience involving a serious illness of his young daughter that he understood the meaning of loneliness. He tells about the extreme loneliness he observed in other children, hospitalized and alone.

Why parents typically are not allowed to stay with their hospitalized children is a puzzle. After all, most parents take care of their children when they have contagious diseases, including the flu. Moreover, most adults have become immune to childhood diseases. And even if the parents do catch, say, the flu from their child, the illness is less traumatic for them and the child than the anxiety and loneliness caused by separation. Also precautions can be taken if medical personnel are afraid that parents might give the child another disease.

Parents and other primary care givers must not allow medical personnel to tell them that they cannot stay with their young children who need them for emotional support. No one knows the child better than the parent, and other care givers need to understand and appreciate this fact. Parents who have a physician who doesn't understand their needs should find a physician who will listen to them.

There are medical arguments against the practice of allowing parents to stay with their child in these situations, but most of them relate to the convenience of the medical staff rather than to the psychological and emotional well-being of the child and the parents. Not all parents are psychologically or emotionally capable or would even choose to stay with an ill child, but they should be given the option.

Parents not only provide good emotional support for their child but can be a valuable asset to the nurses. Parents can comfort a child in pain, give him or her a drink of water or some ice, help with meals, entertain the child while recovering, and in general give the child all but the medical care. Some nurses recognize the help parents can give and appreciate it. Others think parents overprotective and in the way. Pediatric wards should take advantage of this resource; some do.

A child who cries for "mommy" or "daddy" at 2 A.M. will not be comforted as much by a nurse as by a parent. A hospitalized child is in a stressful situation and needs all the support possible. Medical personnel and parents must be sensitive to these emotional requirements. They need to accommodate these needs if they are to help prevent feelings of anxiety and loneliness during these traumatic times.

Most parents appreciate the needs of a hospitalized child and make sacrifices to be with their children. They may have to travel long distances to stay with a sick child. Some have to be absent from their jobs and other children to be with the hospitalized child. But they are willing to make the sacrifices for what they think is important to their child's welfare.

But other parents don't appreciate the needs of a hospitalized young child. When they visit their child, they may greet him or her with, "I can't stay very long; I have so many other things to do" and then spend the time there reading the newspaper rather than interacting with the child. Often in this situation, the child pays no more attention to the parent than the parent pays to him or her. These children learn early and well to cope with their loneliness. This is a classic example of the detachment syndrome. Children appear to accept the situation and seem to be making a good adjustment. Their behavior may, however, be a sign of poor adjustment and apathetic submission.

The stress and loneliness associated with necessary hospitalization of the young child can be reduced. Children who must be hospitalized and their parents can make several visits to the hospital to become familiar with it so it will not be strange when they have to stay there. Parents should stay with the child during the hospitalization, sleeping overnight too. If the hospital staff will not allow them to room in with the child, they should look for a hospital that will accommodate their request or ask their physician to intervene. A parent's presence will help to minimize the fears the child has of medical procedures. Other family members should visit every day to assure the child and to give welcome relief to the rooming-in parent.

Children who have been provided with pleasant separations from parents, such as being left with relatives, grandparents, or other close family friends, are less likely to suffer stress from the trip to the hospital.

## Preschool Child

In one study of loneliness and children, graduate student Carol Travis found that the preschool child (ages 3–5) does understand and experience loneliness but not to the extent anticipated or found at other stages of the life cycle. Eighty-four percent of these children said that loneliness was a sad or bad feeling. Only 9 percent said that it was a good feeling. They said that absence of parents, special friends, and playmates and being alone made them feel lonely. These preschool children defined loneliness as "when you're all alone," "nobody to play with," "when all the lights go out; when you go to bed; when mommy and daddy go," "when you're in bed by yourself."

To determine the loneliness of these children, questionnaires were given to the parents and the nursery school teachers, and a projective test was administered to the children.

The test showed pictorial situations where the child could "project," or reveal feelings of loneliness or of not being lonely. The pictures were designed to be as neutral a stimulus to the child as possible. An example of one picture is a small child standing beside a teenage girl, looking out the window at a car parked a short distance away. The car door is open, and two adults, a male and female, are standing beside the car. The woman is waving. When asked to tell something about this picture, a lonely child might say, "Mommy and daddy are leaving and I have to stay with a baby sitter and that's no fun." A not so lonely child would probably say something like, "Mommy and daddy are leaving and now I can have a lot of fun with the baby sitter."

The findings revealed a great deal. For example, it made no difference in degree of loneliness for these children whether they had regular playmates, slept alone in a room, had a regular babysitter, had make-believe friends, had brothers and sisters, or were male or female. And there was no relationship between loneliness and number of regular playmates, amount of time parents spend with their children, number of instances of loneliness at bedtime, amount of time left alone with a babysitter when the child was awake, age of the parents, and age of the child.

The results of the teacher questionnaire did indicate a significant relationship between loneliness and the time these children spent playing alone at nursery school. Children who spent much of their time playing alone, as measured by the teacher's observations, were the loneliest.

All of the children in this study were attending a university child development laboratory and were from middle- and upper middle-class homes. In general, they were a well-adjusted group with low loneliness scores. Since the variation or range of scores was small, differentiating the more lonely from the less lonely for comparison was difficult. In general, the parents were college graduates and showed great interest in the development of their children. Clearly these children had already learned how to cope in situations with potential for loneliness. And it is hoped that their adjustments were positive and not indifference or detachment.

Children who have to contend with separation, divorce, frequent moving, parental death, alcoholic or drug-abusing parents, poverty, indifference, neglect, abuse, or prejudice must learn methods of survival early. Sometimes their adjustment is not positive.

The research, the literature, personal observation, and experience indicate that the greatest threat to a child's feeling of well-being is separation from their primary support system, the parents. This separation anxiety is the greatest cause of feelings of loneliness. In Travis's research project, she found the greatest number of lonely responses were given to a projective picture where the child is left with a sitter. (Loneliness caused by separation from those we love is not unique to this period in life. It occurs throughout life.)

Some young children left by a parent at nursery school or day care for the first time may cry or throw a tantrum. This is usually followed by a period best described as depression. After a short period of time, the child begins to enter into the school activities, apparently well adjusted to the situation. When the parent arrives to pick up the child, a very interesting thing may happen: the same child who could not bear to have the parent leave a few hours earlier ignores him or her completely. This same child may march into the school the next day without so much as a backward glance. An observer may conclude that the child is making a good adjustment, when in fact it can be a poor one. (This same behavior can be observed in older children and even in some adults.) The child is coping with what he or she views as abandonment, by detaching. A child who continues to adjust in this way may never be able to form strong attachment relationships, thinking, "If I don't get involved, I can't be abandoned."

Some parents try to "sneak" off from their children when it is necessary to leave them, saying that the children will scream if they know that they are being left. But it is better for children to have a tantrum than to have to adjust to never knowing when the parent is about to abandon them.

There are ways to help children adjust to necessary separations. First, parents need to prepare their children for the fact that there will be separations. Then they need to take steps to get children used to a sitter. The first time a sitter comes, for example, the parent should stay in the home while the sitter is there but have the sitter assume the care of the child while doing other things in the house. The parent can gradually leave the house for short periods of time and increase the frequency and the time as the child adjusts to parental absence.

The same procedure should be followed when leaving a child in a church nursery, a sitter's home, or some other child care facility. The parent may have to stay with the child for a period of time at first and then gradually decrease this time until he or she can leave. The parent should assure the child that he or she will be back rather than leave without saying anything. The more secure the child feels, the fewer problems he or she will have. In other words, children will learn to trust parents who are honest with them and don't sneak off.

Parents can also take the child with them when shopping, an experience that helps the child get used to other people while still in the secure care of the parent.

Kahlil Gibran said, "Love knows not its depths until the hour of parting." So it is with loneliness.

# 3

# Adolescents and Young Adults

OH to be young again, laments the poet and others who are over thirty. If they are not just talking about their physical bodies, they must be out of their collective minds. How soon many forget the torture, the anguish, the misery, and the agony that pervade the adolescent years. If adolescence is such a great time in life, why does repeated research find that adolescents are the loneliest group, and why do so many teenagers choose death over life?

## Suicide

Suicide is the second only to accidents as the leading cause of death among young people. The suicide rate for teens and young adults has doubled in the past ten years and tripled in the last twenty. It has been estimated that each year, more than 200,000 young adults contemplate suicide. National statistics indicate that 5,000 adolescent suicide attempts are successful. The actual number may be higher. Police officers report that at least some of the one-car smashups and other kinds of accidents involving teenagers are probably suicides. A driver who crashes a car traveling at high speed into the only tree near the highway for miles around is committing a deliberate act. These events are reported as accidents because of social and family pressures.

Recently four teenagers in New Jersey got together and killed themelves. A few days later, two teenagers took their own lives in copy-cat fashion in Chicago. It appears that these deaths were the result of a suicide pact. In the New Jersey town, several recent deaths reported as accidental are now going to be investigated more thoroughly. Many people in the community, including the mother of one of the victims, consider these "accidents" to be suicides.

Why do these young people choose such a permanent solution to temporary problems? There are a number of theories about this complex problem. One is that teenagers do not yet fully understand the finality of death. Many have not yet experienced the death of a friend, a family member, or a pet. It is doubtful that these adolescents even understand death from an intellectual point of view, and most of them have not experienced it emotionally. We do our best to protect our young people from death.

It is difficult to believe that all of these young people attempting suicide want to die. Only one of every seven of these attempts is successful, compared to one of every two attempts for adults. What they really want is to change their lives for the better, to stop the pain. They are looking for attention, and attempts at suicide usually get them plenty of attention. The problem is that a miscalculation in attempting such a serious act may cost an adolescent his or her life, and in a distraught mental state, it is easy to miscalculate.

Teenagers often think they are surrounded by a protective magic shield. They seem to think that they are not subject to the natural rules and physical laws that control the rest of the world. The teenage girl thinks she won't get pregnant; others think that they can't get killed driving a car at 100 miles an hour on the highway or get hooked on drugs or alcohol.

It would be difficult, if not impossible, to demonstrate a causal relationship between loneliness and suicide, the ultimate withdrawal from a painful experience. But probably a relationship exists. All research studies show that adolescence is the loneliest stage of life. A recent study of rural adolescents found that of 383 teens, 24 (6 percent) said that they "often" or "almost always" felt that their life was not useful. An additional 45 (12 percent) said they felt this way "sometimes." Ten percent said they "often" or "almost always" felt that they did not have much to be proud of or sometimes thought they were no good at all.

A second theory holds that suicide is not the wish for death but a desire to end the unbearable pain, physical or emotional, of life. It is thought that adolescents who find life so intolerable are lonely, alienated and isolated. If this view is accepted, then society must strive to help people find ways to reduce the pain they suffer.

Parents, friends, and teachers of adolescents must be aware of the danger signs of suicide. A suicidal individual begins to withdraw from close friends and family. He or she may be preoccupied with death, life in the hereafter, or even with suicide. There will be problems in school, work, and social activities. Moodiness, appearance of malaise, emptiness, depression, boredom, apathy, an unkempt appearance, or a neglect of personal habits are other symptoms. He or she may give away possessions, especially coveted ones. There may be the onset of alcohol or drug abuse. And there may be change in any of the routine habits that suggest regularity, such as eating and sleeping, and the time of these activities.

Anyone who sees these symptoms should talk to the person and confront him or her about these changes. If the adolescent reveals he or she is thinking about suicide, refuse to keep the secret; tell someone who can help. Many teenagers report after the suicide of a friend that they were afraid the friend would do that but they had been sworn to secrecy by the victim. Unfortunately, sometimes the script is written, and there is little anyone can do about it.

## Challenges of Adolescence

Adolescence, of course, is a special stage in life and can be wonderful. One research project found that 285 of the 383 adolescent subjects (74 percent) "rarely" or "never" felt that they did not have much to be proud of or were no good at all. Adolescence is a period of life from which fabulous memories are made. On balance, to be a teenager is terrific. The majority of teenagers are well adjusted, have normal relationships, are not abnormally lonely, and in general are having a good time. But there are some special challenges during this period of life, perhaps even a few more than at other times.

During this stage of striving for autonomy, peer attachments begin to become primary relationships. As the child develops physically, mentally, and morally, peer relationships replace parent-child attachments as the most influential relationships in the adolescent's life. As adolescents struggle to acquire self-confidence and social abilities that will enable them to establish and maintain these new peer relationships, they are faced with numerous expectations, both their own and those of society. Most achieve less than the expected number and type of these sought-after relationships, and this can be a lonely time. Breaking away from family without having a fairly complete network of friendships already established is difficult.

Each adolescent and his or her parents will handle the separation and loneliness differently. Often adolescents begin to display behaviors and attitudes that surprise and worry the parents; how they handle the changes can significantly affect the future of the parent-child relationship. Parental letting go too soon or too late can add stress, insecurity, dependence, and loneliness in the adolescent. Some children either refuse to or are not allowed to grow up.

The pressure to conform to fad and popular group behavior in order to be popular is sometimes overwhelming. Having the right number of equally popular friends and frequent dates are ideals often tied to an adolescent's sense of self-esteem. The need to be accepted and to be popular with their own social crowd often drives young people to do some risky things. This is a confusing and frightening time, with many options. The need to be accepted at almost any cost removes the focus from the real challenges and developmental goals for this age group, which are to acquire the confidence and social skills necessary to develop satisfying social relationships with people one is interested in, not just the popular crowd, and to possess a strong sense of self that helps to identify important and realistic expectations.

This phase in human development doesn't have the corner on problems. The difficulty here is that adolescents are probably not as well equipped, through experience, to handle problems as well as older age groups are. How often have we all said, "If I just knew then what I know now" or "If I just had that to do over again, I would know better"? Clearly experience helps at any age. Most adults would love to have the physical body and some of the carefree fun they had as a teenager, but as for the rest of it, they would say, "Who needs it?"

When the study of loneliness began several years ago, the researchers did not expect that the adolescent group would be found to be the loneliest, as it was. The elderly were expected to top the list and the adolescent group to be somewhere far down the line. A lot of other people—scientists and lay people alike—didn't believe these findings either. In fact, there was a lot of disbelief and some criticism.

A newspaper reporter doing a feature story on loneliness had heard about the loneliness research and wanted some information for it. The material was provided, and later a copy of the published article was sent to the researchers. When they read the story, they were shocked.

The reporter had taken the material from the loneliness research project and interviewed others to see what they thought about the findings. What she found was interesting. Professional people (who ought to know better or at least be open-minded on the subject) tended to dismiss or ignore the findings on teenage loneliness. A Protestant chaplain and parent who didn't believe the findings about teenagers being the loneliest group observed that teenagers feel everything so intensely that loneliness is only momentary. A psychiatrist made the same conclusion. He indicated that since young people have their whole future before them, they can hope for things to get better if their present hopes are smashed. He said that they may feel a present loneliness, but that is all it is. He thought that the middle aged are more clearly the lonely. If they have shattered dreams, there isn't much future left for them to pick up the pieces. Another woman interviewed said that she thought the researchers were, among other things, "all wet." She based this opinion on her experience with her own three teenage daughters and the elderly with whom she worked.

## High School Students

Beverly Otto, one of the researchers, completed a project that examined loneliness among freshman and senior students in selected rural high schools. Her conclusion was that adolescents are the loneliest group, with rural senior high school girls the loneliest of them all.

Otto administered the Loneliness Inventory, the Personal Information Questionnaire, and the Self-Esteem Questionnaire to 382 senior high school students in four selected rural towns in Nebraska with populations of 1500 to 2500. For both the freshman and senior students, she found that girls were significantly lonelier than boys and that there was a relationship between loneliness and self-esteem; the higher was the self-esteem score, the less lonely was the student.

For the freshman class, "ease in making friends" and "availability of transportation" were important factors in coping with loneliness. Freshmen who reported that it was "almost always easy to make friends" were the least lonely. Number of close friends did not make any difference. For these students, loneliness scores increased as transportation became more difficult.

The real surprise was to find that those participating in three to five extracurricular activities were significantly lonelier than those participating in only one. Follow-up interviews indicated that adolescents who engaged in fewer activities were committed to them. Many of the lonelier adolescents were not committed to any one activity.

Religion did not make a difference in loneliness. For freshmen, the trend was that those who practiced no religion were found to be the least lonely. The next lowest loneliness category was for those who were other than Protestant, Catholic, or Jewish. Seniors who chose the "other" category were the least lonely. Religious worship service attendance was not related to loneliness.

A recent study of rural Nebraska adolescents living on a farm or ranch or in a small town (population under 2500) found high loneliness scores for this group. These rural adolescents' loneliness scores were exceeded only by those of urban high school girls.

The general findings of this study indicate that the rural adolescent who was significantly less lonely was a male; lived on a farm or ranch or in a town of less than 1000 population; lived more than fifteen miles from the nearest town; visited with friends on the telephone only once a week or not at all (those who visited two to six times a week or once a day were the loneliest); had a greater number of close friends; enjoyed a "very close" relationship with his or her parents (45 percent did); reported "very close" and "very distant" relationships with siblings; did not pick a day of the week or a season of the year as being the loneliest; "often" or "almost always" took a positive attitude toward self; and had high self-esteem. These characteristics are also true for females; it just happens that males are significantly less lonely than females.

In a study of urban high school senior girls over a period of four years, John Woodward found these adolescents to be the loneliest of all the groups studied. They were expected to have high loneliness scores but not higher than those of the rural adolescent senior high school girls.

## College Students

Leaving home and/or leaving one's home town for college is an experience similar to the breaking away that occurs in adolescence. Young adults are many times launched into a town to begin anew without the accustomed comforts of home, friends, and family. Their high school reputation and status are gone. In a sense, they are at ground zero. They must start all over again in establishing friendships, romantic relationships, and support networks including mentors.

As early as 1959, psychologist S. Schacter found that people seek companionship in frightening or anxious circumstances; this type of stress may increase the desire or need to affiliate. Beginning college in a new town, with strangers, in new and potentially threatening situations such as not being in familiar surroundings, eating meals alone in crowded dining halls, and final exams, do indeed cause a yearning for companionship.

The first year in this new world of independence and higher education is often a time of intense loneliness. These feelings can lead a student to drop out and return home to the security of familiar faces and places. Others may suffer academically, go to great lengths to be in social situations (constant partying), or even resort to suicide. In 1979, Carolyn Cutrona and Letitia Peplau found that, in general, a student's attitude was a much better predictor of later recovery from loneliness than was reported social behavior. Those with high expectations for future relationships were less lonely at the end of one year than those who told themselves that they really did not need a lot of friends or a dating partner and gave up. One point to note, however, was that decreases in loneliness were not strongly associated with increases in contact with friends but instead with increases in satisfaction with friends. Working to deepen and enrich relationships with new acquaintances is important in overcoming feelings of loneliness.

Through research conducted in 1980 by Daniel Russell, Letitia Peplau and Carolyn Cutrona, a picture of the lonely college student comes into focus. Typically this individual lacks self-confidence, is sensitive to rejection, and is unassertive. Each of these factors contributes to an inability to initiate social relationships and thus affects the process of adapting to a new social environment.

Additional pressures on college students include stereotypes that indicate more is better—for example, that the more social relationships, including dates and friends, that one has, the better. Most current research suggests, however, that satisfaction with relationships, not frequency of social contacts, is directly related to staving off loneliness. Cutrona and Peplau found also that it was satisfaction with current friendships that predicted low loneliness scores, not satisfaction with dating or family relationships.

Not only are different relationships important in relieving loneliness, but different relationships meet different psychological needs. Robert Weiss, a sociologist, refers to them as "a basic set of 6 provisions provided by social relationships." For example, friendship commonly provides feelings of sharing similar concerns and activities. Intimate relationshps, such as with a spouse or other romantic partner, fulfill attachment, security, and commitment needs. Family relationships fulfill needs for continuity and reliability. Colleagues help to provide "reassurance of worth by valuing our work contributions. And mentors offer guidance and nurturance."

Researcher Shirley Seevers studied loneliness that college freshmen experienced. She examined gender, the practice of a religious faith and church attendance, residential location (rural or urban during childhood), father's occupation, family income, adequacy of present income of student, mother's employment during the student's childhood, childhood happiness, selected family relationships, selected peer relationships, dating status of student, homesickness experienced by student, and extracurricular activities participated in by student. Three hundred and forty-five college freshman students responded to the Loneliness Inventory and a demographic questionnaire. The variables found to be significantly related to loneliness were similar to Otto's research of senior high school students. The important variables were gender (females were lonelier than males); practicing membership in a religious faith (those who practiced no religious faith or one other than Judaism, Catholicism, or Protestantism, had the lowest loneliness scores); ease in making friends (the easier it was to make friends, the less lonely was the student); and homesickness (the more frequently the freshman experienced homesickness, the lonelier was the student).

An interesting finding was that church attendance was not related to loneliness. It seemed possible that the more an adolescent went to a church or synagogue, the less lonely he or she would be. Equally interesting, those who practiced one of the recognized faiths were lonelier than those who practiced no religious faith at all. When this is all put together, however, it does make sense. The major factor contributing to this result is selectivity. As a group, those who attend religious services tend to be lonelier and seek ways to relieve their loneliness. Individuals who do not attend these services or belong to organized religious groups are not as lonely.

In a 1983 study, researchers Nilufer Medora and John Woodward found that there had not been any real changes in the loneliness picture for college students from a 1972 study done by Shirley Seevers. The loneliness scores of college students were slightly, but not significantly, lower than those students in the earlier study. The characteristics found related to loneliness were gender (females were lonelier than males); ease in making friends (students who found it easy to make friends were the least lonely, even though the number of close friends made no difference); and self-rated happiness (those who said that they had been "very happy" or "happy" during the past year had the lowest loneliness scores and the "unhappy" and "very unhappy" the highest). Also found was a direct relationship between how the students rated themselves and their loneliness scores. Those who described themselves as "the most lonely person they knew" were the loneliest, followed by, in descending order, "more lonely than most people," "about as lonely," and "less lonely."

There appears to be no relationship between loneliness and socioeconomic status; church attendance (although not statistically significant, students who attended church once a week or more were lonelier than those who never attended); number of siblings; ordinal position (the oldest and youngest tended to be the loneliest while the least lonely were the middle children); number of close friends; and happiness during childhood.

## Single Adolescent Mothers

In another study researcher Maxine Bauermeister looked at self-esteem and the loneliness of single adolescent mothers with at least one child and living on welfare. Although this adolescent group was found to have high loneliness scores, they were not as high as those of several other adolescent groups. In this study, two factors contributed to feelings of loneliness: the fact that they were adolescents and that they had special problems.

This research found that adolescents who had completed high school and those enrolled in postsecondary education were less lonely than those who had completed ninth, tenth, or eleventh grades (this finding is probably related to another that younger subjects were somewhat lonelier than older subjects). The adolescent mothers whose own parents were still married and living together were less lonely than those whose families were no longer intact. There was a relationship between availability of transportation and loneliness; those with transportation problems were lonelier. And the higher was the monthly income, the less lonely was the adolescent mother. Frequency of church attendance was not related to feelings of loneliness.

A project closely related to Otto's and Bauermeister's research was completed by Judith Bucklin Joern. Her study was with loneliness among low-income single-parent mothers. Although their average age, 25.9, is probably better described as young adult, in many ways, these subjects displayed characteristics typical of adolescent subjects.

The subjects for this research were single-parent mothers defined as separated, deserted, divorced, widowed, or never married. All of the participants in the study were recipients of some county welfare assistance in the form of Aid to Dependent Children (ADC). They had at least one preschool child at home. Thirty percent of these mothers had never been married, 18 percent were separated, 51 percent were divorced, and 1 percent had been deserted. Over half the mothers (56 percent) were employed or in educational programs that required them to be away from home for a major portion of the day; therefore they had to arrange for child care. A personal information questionnaire and the Loneliness Inventory were administered to these subjects.

The low-income single-parent mothers who were found to be significantly less lonely had transportation available and had not received personal counseling regarding their single parenthood. This latter finding may appear surprising; it means that those who have had or who are in counseling are the loneliest. But because individuals who seek counseling are the ones who are the loneliest and need help, the results are not so surprising as they may initially appear.

Additional findings indicated that the parent who was significantly lonelier was very concerned about the conflict between dating and parenting, felt that society frowns upon single-parent families, and did not feel self-reliant.

## Adolescents with Physical Impairments

An interesting project that has made a significant contribution to the overall loneliness project and adolescent research was completed by Delores Gladbach. Her study was concerned with loneliness among selected adolescents with physical impairments. The majority of the subjects in her study were impaired with cerebral palsy, although there were some individuals with paraplegia, quadriplegia, and muscular dystrophy. The Loneliness Inventory and Self-Esteem Questionnaire were again used in this research proejct. Of all the variables studied, Gladbach found that only gender and self-esteem made a difference. Females were lonelier than males, and as self-esteem scores increased, loneliness scores decreased.

There were some surprises. Results from the Self-Esteem Questionnaire indicated that this group had high self-esteem; very few of the subjects indicated that they felt inferior. On the contrary, they scored well above average for level of self-confidence and positive attitude toward self. On the whole, they had adjusted well to their life situation. The majority considered their family relationships to be "very close," their childhood to have been "very happy" or "happy," and their present feelings of happiness to be "very happy" or "happy." None of these adolescents indicated unhappiness or discontent.

This was not the only surprising finding. These adolescents, although lonelier than the adult groups, were one of the least lonely adolescent groups. The prediction had been that this group would be the loneliest of the adolescent groups, based on the old stereotype that an individual confined to a wheelchair would have no friends and would be unable to do anything that would relieve feelings of loneliness. The error in predicting the correct level of their loneliness was in underestimating the resoucefulness of these individuals and their care givers. Another important factor is that these adolescents also require nearly constant care. Thus someone is with them, or not too far away, almost all of the time.

Support for this line of reasoning is found in a research project conducted by Joyce Donlan, this concerning loneliness among hemophiliacs. Donlan found these adolescents to score even slightly lower than those in Gladbach's study. Because of necessity, these individuals receive a lot of care and concern. Donlan asked them: "What good things have come into your life because of hemophilia?" One of the subjects said, "My daddy pays more attention to me than he does to my brothers or sisters." Another answered, "I got to go to Los Angeles to the hospital." "I get a lot of attention."

## Causes of Adolescent Loneliness

What does the research indicate about adolescents and loneliness? Why are adolescents the loneliest of all the groups studied? What are the causes, and what are the cures? Why are young women lonelier than young men?

The research reveals a great deal about the relationship or the lack of relationship between loneliness and other factors in the adolescent's life. There are no cures for loneliness, but by looking at these relationships perhaps some conclusions can be reached or at least a better understanding of the causes can be formulated. If the impact of some of the causes can be removed or reduced, some of the feelings of loneliness can be relieved.

First, why are adolescents lonelier than all the other groups? Many look at adolescence as a crisis period, and for good reason. Experts in human behavior have always viewed this period of transition from childhood to adulthood as one of storm and stress. Some have described it as a time of turmoil, of searching for one's identity, of self-doubt, alienation, apprehension, anxiety, insecurity, and suffering. It has also been described as a stage for idealism, new self-awareness, establishing a unique identity, defining moral and ethical values, and becoming independent.

According to anthropologists, these are not universal phenomena. In some societies, the period of adolescence may transpire without much notice. In primitive societies, and in some instances in our own, the teenage years pass as a smooth transition from childhood to adulthood. Some explain that the disturbance observed is related to the physiological changes that take place during this time. The difficulty with that explanation is that the psychological problems don't usually occur until after the physical changes have occurred. Instead, a lot of adolescence is cultural. It is extolled, glorified, and amplified today, not the least by the media.

Fifty years ago, the biggest change that took place during adolescence was that you didn't have to wear long underwear in the winter anymore and you got your driver's license. Now most kids don't wear long underwear unless they are going on a ski trip, and then it's thermal. Getting a driver's license is still an important ritual and a thrill, but it is not the same. Now it is much more associated with becoming independent: "Now Mom doesn't have to drive me, and I can run all sorts of errands for myself." In the past, getting a license was not so much independence as a simple achievement.

Being a teenager today is probably more stressful than it was in an earlier time. Teenagers are bombarded with pressures from their friends and the media to participate in activities considered immoral in a less permissive society of yesterday. The moral values popularized by television and the movies about sex, alcohol, and drugs would lead one to believe that to be different is old-fashioned. The media have turned around the old story—"Boy meets girl, boy falls in love with girl, boy marries girl and they live happily ever after"—to "Boy meets girl, they jump into bed, and they may never see one another again." The pressure to conform and participate, in spite of wanting desperately to hold on to more conservative values, may be too much for the vulnerable teenager.

Never before have there been so many publications devoted to the teenagers or to the parents of teenagers. Magazines such as *Seventeen*, *Teenage*, and *ym* ("your magazine") are written especially for adolescent girls. In a recent ad, one of these publishers said that the magazine "helps you get it all together, makes being a teen more fun." Articles in these magazines discuss such topics as getting boys to like you, to rush or not rush, how to become more popular, bringing out the best in yourself, sixteen new hair styles, and even loneliness.

The reason for this media hype is obvious: the size of the adolescent market. Today's teenagers appear to have a lot of freedom and seem to control a great deal of money and credit. Parents are implored by creditors to allow teenagers to have credit cards. They are told that it is important so that young people can achieve independence, learn to manage their money, and in case of emergency have this resource for help. Certainly some of these objectives are persuasive and have some validity. Most parents can see through to the real reasons, however. On balance, plastic credit may contribute positively to the teenager's life and to the life of everyone else. It certainly contributes heavily to the national economy. There seems to be a national obsession with youth. Not only the media but now the creditors want a piece of the action. Is it no wonder that teenagers have problems with trying to live up to all these expectations and become depressed and lonely?

The media set up a tremendous expectancy. When the individual expects a lot and does not fulfill that expectancy, he or she is probably going to become depressed and lonely. Why should inexperienced adolescents expect anything less than perfect relationships when, for the most part, all they see on television are fantastic relationships between beautiful people? It takes a lot of living to realize that you can enjoy relationships that are less than perfect with less than beautiful people. Although relationships are the most important factor as far as loneliness is concerned, the expectancy doesn't end here. "Bill Cosby always seems to have time to discuss the latest crises with his children. Why can't we have a perfect family like that?" "Everyone on TV seems to be so much more beautiful, rich, famous, and always having so much more fun and excitement than I am."

At this time of life, decision making is important. And it is a lonely process. No one else can do it for you. Adolescents lack experience in the decision-making process. Starting in the junior year of high school and intensifying in the senior year, the student has to make some important decisions concerning the next phase of life. Should I go to college? If I decide to go to college, which one is best for me? What area of study should I choose? What courses should I take? Each decision branches into the need to make more decisions. If I choose a college, what dorm should I live in? What about a roommate? Should I go through rush, and if I get a bid should I pledge? And this is only part of the college educational decision process. What about all the other educational choices? Those who have made these decisions or who are in the process of making them can appreciate the stress and the loneliness accompanying the decision making.

Adolescents need to be allowed to make their own decisions and their own mistakes. An adolescent who finds that he or she has made a wrong decision cannot blame the parent. He or she cannot hide frustrations by saying, "I never wanted to go there in the first place. You made the choice; I didn't." Parents do need to be sympathetic and supportive. They should not say, "It was your choice; don't blame me." What they should say is, "We all make mistakes, and we need to learn from them." And they should help children recover from their wrong decisions with understanding and patience. How else will they learn?

Adolescents have other decisions to make: about jobs, marriage and other personal relationships, moral and ethical values, where they are going to live, and on and on.

Adolescents who decide to leave home and go away to college or to another city to take a job have separated themselves from their primary support systems. Their parents and other loved ones, their long-time friends, and their teachers are no longer around to help them with their problems and to help them relieve the feelings of loneliness. They have to establish new relationships and support systems, not always an easy task. Remember that ease of making friends is an important factor in coping with loneliness. Not everyone has this ability. They have to establish what might be called their credibility. Since everyone at home—their parents, friends, teachers, and others—has always known them, they didn't have to worry about making impressions. An example might be the excellent student in high school who goes away to college. All the high school teachers knew this student, and the student knew all the teachers and what they expected. Now in college, this student has to reestablish the fact that he or she is an excellent student. There is no more depending on reputation. This can be a lonely experience—or an opportunity for the not-so-good student to do better.

## Understanding and Coping

It is now known that adolescence is the loneliest time in the developmental periods of the life cycle. Many of the factors associated with loneliness and adolescence are also known. The next logical step after the awareness and understanding is to develop ways to help adolescents cope with these feelings.

An important concept for everyone to understand is that to be lonely is normal. It is part of the human condition and is especially true for adolescents. Many adolescents are afraid that their feelings of loneliness are abnormal, and this increases the problem.

One mother said that her teenage daughter who was away in college frequently called home in tears because she was so homesick and lonely. She told her mother that she didn't understand why she was the only one who felt that way. She said that she hid in the bathroom to cry because she didn't want anyone to see her. Her mother was familiar with the loneliness research and was able to assure her daughter that her feelings were very normal and that many others were hiding their feelings too. She told her that she needed to reach out to other students, to be honest and to share her feelings with them. She could also share her problems with dorm counselors and professors. In this way, others would share their feelings with her. The mother related that her daughter did find out that others were having the same problems. Finding out that she was "normal" not only reduced the anxiety of the daughter but of the mother as well.

Adolescents need to reach out to others to relieve their feelings of loneliness. They have to share their feelings so that others in turn will share their feelings with them.

Adults can help adolescents develop skills in making friends. It is this ability—not the number of friends one has—that is crucial in warding off loneliness.

The ability to make friends begins with the development of self-esteem. Research has shown that adolescents with low self-esteem tend to be lonely, and they cope by putting up a false front of detachment or aloofness. This is their way of trying to convince others that they are too busy for activities or interactions while they retreat into their own world of loneliness. People who do not have a good opinion of themselves and do not become involved cannot expect others to want to be their friend. Greater self-esteem enables people to develop their ability to make friends and in turn become less lonely.

Self-acceptance is crucial to high self-esteem. The title of psychologist Jess Lair's book, *I Aint Much, Baby—But I'm All I've Got*, says a lot. We can't be someone else—the pop singer we adore or the movie hero we idolize. We have to work with what we have. Only by self-acceptance can we become the person we want to be.

To begin this process, take an inventory. Write down everything you like about yourself. Be honest; you might be surprised. Then write down everything you dislike. Next develop a plan to strengthen your strong points and your positive but weak areas and change the things you don't like about yourself. Then work at the plan. This will not be easy, but most things that are worthwhile take time and effort.

Get paper and pencil and stand in front of a full-length mirror. Take a good long look at yourself and write down all the positives and negatives. If your appearance satisfies you, fine, but if you don't like some of the things you see: your weight, shape, hair, clothes, eyeglasses, or even the color of your eyes, you can do something about it. Now sit down and take stock of your school life. Are you happy with your grades, the classes you take, the educational goals you have set for yourself? Examine your friendships. Are you satisfied with your relationships or are there some improvements you can make? Maybe you need to make new friends. Most important, think about your family members and your interactions with them. Are you pleased with your relationships or are there some things you can do to improve them? Finally, set up a plan to do something about each area. This is the only way you can come to accept and improve yourself so that you can be the person you really want to be.

You will be pleased with the results. As you begin to feel good about yourself, others will feel good about you too. You will gain the self-confidence it takes to make friends and relieve your feelings of loneliness.

# 4

# The Middle Years

FEW think that life waits until forty to begin, but they do believe that the middle years are the best of their lives. In general, the middle years are the most productive, the years of greatest accomplishments, and where one's monuments (those things that will outlive you), including children, are created. Generally people in their middle years have achieved some financial security, have established themselves professionally and socially, and are in the prime of life.

But this period, like any other, has problems. Many middle-aged people feel trapped between their children and their aging parents—part of what some have called the sandwich generation. They find themselves caught between educational responsibilities to their children and care for their aging parents. The ever-increasing costs in both of these areas can constitute a real challenge. Returning children also can cause problems. Just when the parents think that they have their children educated and launched into careers and marriage, the children are back—sometimes because of divorce, problems with job, or need for further support because of graduate education. And when loneliness strikes in middle age, it is usually associated with a period of personal crisis.

When does middle age begin? Almost everyone has his or her own answer to that question. At a college departmental meeting some time ago, a proposal for a new course, "The Middle Years," was introduced. The first question was, "What years will this cover?" When the answer was the years between 30 and 60, the staff members who were about to turn 30 or who were just a few years over 30 almost started a riot. They weren't even nice about it, and they were serious. Those in the meeting who were moving toward 60 and those slightly on the other side did not take it any better. The course was finally approved, but the staff never did reach a consensus on the years to be covered by the middle years course. When it is taught, the definition probably depends on the age of the instructor.

## Divorce

There are slightly more divorces during this period than at any other. Like death, divorce, a period of crisis, can bring about a sudden and sometimes unwanted loss of relationship. The shock of this lost relationship, whether wanted or unwanted, can lead to feelings of loneliness. One recently divorced woman said that she thought the death of a spouse must be easier. She said, "I am still in love with my former husband, and when I see him with others and I can't be a part of it, it really bothers me. I can hardly stand it. At least when a spouse leaves through death, you are generally left with better memories than with a divorce." She continued, "My former husband is in the same town, and as long as he is around to remind me, it is going to be hard for me to get on with my life."

The research concerned with loneliness and the middle years began with a project on loneliness and divorce completed by Jackie Zabel. Recent studies indicate that her findings are as applicable today as they were then. No matter how sophisticated people think society is today, divorce is not much easier than it was twenty years ago. The feelings and emotions of the individuals involved didn't go away. Although some progress has been made, the negative attitudes toward divorce have not changed much.

Zabel administered the Loneliness Inventory and a personal

data questionnaire to a group of divorced men and women and found them to be among the lonelier adults. The average length of time the males had been divorced was 2 years and 5.5 for the females. The average age of the males was 33 and of the females 38.6.

The research showed that women were lonelier than men, especially when they were in social situations where people thought less of them after finding out that they were divorced. Both men and women felt extreme loneliness when they were left out or rejected by others, although neither felt loneliness in relation to feelings of rejection by family. Both groups experienced significant loneliness when they felt out of place at a particular time or event because they were divorced. When finances became a problem, women were very lonely, much more so than men. And women expressed greater feelings of loneliness than men when decisions had to be made, and they had no one with whom to share the responsibility. Women were also lonely when they wanted to join an activity and were unable to do so. Women more than men felt loneliness when there were daily tasks to perform and no one with whom to share the responsibilities. In relationship to the divorce process, subjects expressed the greatest feelings of loneliness before the final decree. For men, it was at the first filing and for women the final separation. Neither the presence of children nor their number seemed to affect feelings of loneliness. Whether relatives lived in the same city did not affect loneliness. Although they were a small number, women living with their parents were among the loneliest, and men living with parents had loneliness scores above average.

## Never-Married Persons

Charline Swanson did loneliness research with the never-married. Her subjects were between the ages of 22 and 60 years of age and not engaged in undergraduate college work or special schooling. She administered the Loneliness Inventory and a personal data questionnaire to these individuals. Generally they were not as lonely as she had anticipated; in fact, they were among the least lonely middle-years groups: slightly lonelier than housewives but not very much.

Women were lonelier than men. As age increased, loneliness scores decreased; the 22–30 age group was the loneliest and the 51–60 the least. The happier the subjects had been during the past year, the less lonely they were, and the closer they lived to the parent or parents, the less lonely they were. Religious preference, extent of religious feeling, and church attendance were found not to be related to feelings of loneliness.

## Housewives

Another research project concerned with loneliness in the middle years of life was completed by Mary Jane Visser, who studied urban housewives. The term *housewife* was chosen to differentiate this sample from *homemaker*, which can mean anyone who makes a home; it can thus include single women, divorced women, or men who keep the home. Visser's aim was to study married women taking care of the home. This definition encompassed wives who worked outside the home and those who did not, as well as those who had children and those who did not. The Loneliness Inventory and a personal data questionnaire were used in this study.

Housewives were the least lonely of all the middle-years groups. Visser found that housewives with husbands who had jobs that almost always or often required them to be away from home more than eight hours a day were lonelier than those who were not in this situation. Limited family income and feelings that financial considerations prevented participation in desired activities contributed heavily to feelings of loneliness. Although loneliness was not significantly related to whether the housewife was employed, the employed housewife was somewhat lonelier (45 percent of the women were employed outside the home). Subjects who were discontent with their lives or who felt that the last year had been unhappy were the lonely ones. There was no relationship between the number of social activities in which the housewife participated and loneliness.

## Alcoholics

Nilufer Medora studied loneliness and alcoholism as a period of crisis in the lives of a sample of young adults and individuals in their middle years. Alcoholics were defined as individuals undergoing treatment at an alcoholic treatment center. The Loneliness Inventory, a personal data questionnaire, and self-esteem scale were administered to the subjects.

The alcoholic group attained very high loneliness scores—third highest among the adult groups. There was a very strong relationship between self-esteem and loneliness: alcoholics with low self-esteem were the loneliest. As age increased, loneliness decreased; younger subjects were significantly lonelier than older subjects. Female alcoholics were found to be lonelier than male alcoholics.

The research group consisted of people with an education that ranged all the way from less than high school to the completion of graduate degrees. There was no difference in the feelings of loneliness for these different groups, nor were there differences in scores for the diverse socioeconomic groups or for the groups with various feelings about the adequacy of their income. Alcoholism is obviously the overriding issue. There was no relationship between loneliness and religious preference or frequency of church attendance. Although marital status was not found to be related to loneliness, self-rated marital satisfaction was: individuals who had high self-rated marital satisfaction were less lonely than those who reported that they were not satisfied. Individuals who reported their health to be very poor were lonelier than those who reported their health to be average, good, or excellent.

As with the other groups, the number of close friends was not related to feelings of loneliness but ease in making friends was. The alcoholic who found it easy to make friends was the least lonely. There was also a relationship between job satisfaction and loneliness: those who were dissatisfied with their jobs were much lonelier than those who said they were satisfied. Alcoholics who had a history of alcoholism in their family were significantly lonelier than those who had no such history. A negative relationship was found between the number of years alcohol had been consumed and loneliness. This means that the longer these people had been drinking, the less lonely they were. This finding could be a spurious or deceptive finding because of another factor that probably contributed to both loneliness and how long they had been drinking: age. This research demonstrated that adolescents are lonelier than adults. They have also had less time to drink. In addition, the more experience one has had, the better able one can cope with loneliness.

The next finding was a bit of a surprise: those who said the last year had been "very happy" were the loneliest. This finding, although a reversal from all the other studies, is understandable. The subjects were being asked about the past year, a time when they were still drinking heavily and prior to beginning treatment. Alcoholics have their drinking buddies and become unhappy and lonely when they have to face up to their problem, stop drinking and go into treatment. They are certainly happier drinking or they would stop. This concept is hard for people who have not had to deal with alcoholics to understand. Many counselors believe it to be true nevertheless. When one alcohol rehabilitation counselor was asked, "What is the best thing you can do for an alcoholic?" He said without the least hesitation, "Get them into trouble." He continued: "That may sound harsh, but for some alcoholics that seems to be the only way you can get their attention." They have to become unhappy with themselves, admit that they have a problem, want to do something about their problem, and then do something about it. This perhaps is a good prescription for problems of loneliness too.

## Rural Adults

A recent research project with rural adults living on farms and ranches found that this group was among the loneliest of all the adult groups in the studies. Loneliness and crisis are closely related; many farmers are experiencing crisis because of the depressed farm economy.

Although all subjects expressed feelings of loneliness, the loneliest rural people were women; those living on a rural farm or ranch rather than in a small rural town; under 70 years of age; could not afford everything they wanted; had distant relationships with their parents and brothers and sisters; spent a half a day or more alone each week; consider themselves less than "almost always" happily married; were not satisfied with their job; were not happy about the last year; never, rarely, or only sometimes thought they were in good health; had problems making friends; never, rarely, or only sometimes got out among other adults for social reasons; did not visit with their relatives as often as they would like; were not satisfied with their current life situation; never or rarely visited or talked to relatives who live within fifty miles of their home; remembered the past year as less lonely than the present; and never or rarely entertained friends in their homes.

Some of the items of interest that were not found to be related to loneliness were distance they lived from the nearest town; number of children; how often they visited with friends by phone; how often they attended religious services; and how often they confided in friends about personal matters.

## Care Center Chaplains

The Loneliness Inventory was given to a large group of care center chaplains who worked in hospitals, prisons, rehabilitation centers, retirement homes, county and city shelters for the homeless and runaways, and chemical dependency centers during a loneliness workshop. The chaplains were very interested in the topic and curious about how they would score on the inventory. Some thought that their scores would be very high because of the kind of work they do—counseling the lonely. But they were nevertheless surprised when they did turn out to be a very lonely group. In fact, their scores were the highest recorded for any other adult group.

Some of the chaplains concluded that their scores were probably more indicative of an empathic (compassionate) loneliness than their own feelings. They thought that it was almost impossible for them to answer the questions out of the context of their profession. They felt that their scores were influenced by the desperately lonely people they counseled every day.

Not all of the chaplains agreed with this analysis, but it has some merit. It must be difficult to work constantly with lonely people without becoming immersed in their feelings of loneliness. The compassion and empathy of counselors may have its own price, loneliness. Although these individuals may not be facing personal crisis in their own lives, they face loneliness, despair, heartache, grief, and the sorrow of others on a daily basis.

## Crisis

Research tells us that people do experience loneliness in the middle years more than in later years but not as severely as in the adolescent years. Also, people in the middle years cope relatively well with loneliness except in times of crisis.

Rural adults confronted by the crisis of a depressed farm economy, threatened by the loss of the work of a lifetime, and, for some, the loss of the family farm are not significantly less lonely than the care center chaplains. Many farm people feel manipulated and abandoned by a society they have served so well for hundreds of years. They wonder if this is their thanks for providing food for the country with enough left over to feed the rest of the world.

The alcoholics followed the rural adults in magnitude of loneliness scores. The research on alcoholics and loneliness was done with alcoholics undergoing treatment as in-patients in alcohol rehabilitation centers and thus being forced to face their alcoholism as a problem. Some had entered treatment on their own; others had been forced by the courts, employers, or others. Alcoholism had, by definition, become a crisis in their lives.

Theories abound concerning the causes of alcoholism, all centering around the question of environmental versus hereditary influence. Recent research supporting the theory that alcoholism is a disease with a genetic base is rapidly gaining favor. But even the proponents of the environmental influences for alcoholism are not sure whether loneliness causes alcoholism. It is known that alcoholics are lonely, however.

The divorced individuals were found to be less lonely than the care center chaplains, rural adults, and alcoholics. Nevertheless, divorce is a crisis period in many adult lives. This is especially true during the middle years. These are marriages that typically have lasted a number of years, and children and property are usually involved. All of these factors contribute to the strong feelings of attachment and dependency that make the separation more difficult. No matter how bad the relationship, divorced people say that the losses suffered cause grief, anxiety, and loneliness.

The never-married and housewives were the least lonely in the middle years studies. If the theory holds that loneliness decreases with age after adolescence except in times of crisis, this is to be expected. It would be predicted that these same individuals placed in a crisis situation—grief, alcoholism, financial problems, loss of a significant other such as a close friend or a spouse—would suffer a higher incidence of loneliness.

Isolation, despair, and loneliness drive people to commit desperate acts. A short time ago, a respected, middle-aged professional man, desperate over financial problems, his inability to provide for his family as he wanted to, and faced with the possibility that his wife was about to divorce him, killed his wife and three children before turning the gun on himself. At the memorial service, the minister said, "Beyond the grief of this family tragedy there is a lesson: People must reach out for the help of others in difficult times. When we are troubled and are experiencing frustration and dejection and loneliness, that's the time we have to reach out for others who care about us." Those words provide guidance for all of us in our own loneliness.

One of the important findings of the research for the middle years is that loneliness is normal. This fact serves to assure individuals in this developmental stage, as in other stages, that to be lonely is normal. Too many think that they are the only ones who suffer the pain of loneliness. Once they understand this, they can get on with coping with their loneliness.

It is also known that crisis is the important variable associated with loneliness during this period of life. Whether the crisis is the result of grief over the loss of a loved one through death, divorce, or desertion; loss of a job; relocation; a bad evaluation by a supervisor; or a serious illness is relatively unimportant. The results are the same: loneliness. Developing strategies to deal with crises will help to relieve feelings of loneliness.

## Coping Strategies

Coping strategies for the middle years are similar to those for the adolescent years. Individuals in the middle years need to reach out to others to relieve their feelings of loneliness. They need to turn to family, friends, and others to help them with their problems and to share their feelings. They should not be reluctant to turn to professionals for help when the crisis and the loneliness become too much to endure. When people are physically ill they seldom hesitate to see a physician. When it comes to psychological problems many people are unwilling to admit that they cannot handle their problems alone. These people must overcome the idea that it is a weakness if you can't solve your own personal problems. Yet it is no more a weakness to see a professional counselor about a personal problem than it is to see a physician about a physical problem. When the old home remedies just don't work, get professional help.

# 5

# The Later Years

As life expectancy rates continue to climb, the number of older citizens living in the United States becomes an even larger percentage of the overall population. The Bureau of the Census projects that the number of 100-year-olds in this country is rising so fast that by 1990 there will probably be 50,000, double the current total. By the year 2000, there will be about 100,000 people aged 100 or older. By 2050 there are expected to be about a million centenarians. This number is forty times the number today.

In 1776, the average life expectancy was 33 years for men and 35 for women. A hundred years later, it was up to 42 and 45, respectively. A baby born in the 1980s can expect to live an average of 73.9 years. Male children may expect to live 70.1 and females 77.6 years. Currently the over-55 age group accounts for 21.3 percent and the over-65 age group accounts for 11.9 percent of the total population. These percentages are growing rapidly.

These figures bring up an interesting question: At what age is a person considered old? As with any other age group, everyone has his or her own definition of old. Age is relative, but for the purposes of the loneliness studies, persons 60 years of age and beyond were considered to be older or elderly.

## Golden or Tarnished?

Are the later years golden years, or are they tarnished by loneliness? Through twenty years of researching loneliness in all age groups, the elderly continue to be found to be the least lonely group. Advancing age brings with it a variety of changes and personal losses, but experience gained throughout a lifetime of living and learning brings more effective coping strategies and more realistic expectations.

Today's senior citizens find themselves in a different set of circumstances from those of any prior elderly generation. Three-quarters of today's elderly own their own homes. Many have had an opportunity to plan financially for retirement and save enough to live comfortably. As a group, the elderly are better off financially than they ever were. The mean income for the elderly has gone up at the same time that their poverty rate has gone down.

## Living Alone

There are, however, many elderly, especially widows, living alone and struggling to make ends meet. According to recent census statistics, of the 8 million elderly Americans living alone, 81 percent are widowed and 77 percent are women. The majority (two-thirds) of the elderly live in metropolitan areas, with more than half living in the suburbs as opposed to the central cities. Twenty-five percent live on incomes below the federal poverty line. They are usually widowed, struggling to get from month to month without losing their independence.

Most of these elderly do not see their children and grandchildren often and have some form of illness or disability that limits their independence and physical functioning. With the help of social services aid, most of these people are able to remain in their own home or apartment, although they may need help with cleaning, laundry, shopping, driving, and cooking. In a lot of cases, minor assistance allows these elderly persons to remain in their own surroundings. This means a great deal to them and at the same time saves large amounts of money on nursing home care.

One of the myths of aging is that elderly people do not want to live alone. Contrary to what is popularly believed, only one in one hundred elderly people who live alone actually wants to live with their children. Only one in ten wants to live with someone else. In 1986, more than 8 million of the 28 million people age 65 or older lived alone. Many are quite happy in this situation and have adjusted to not needing the steady companionship of a spouse or roommate. Nevertheless, when one of the marital partners dies, many children begin making plans to move the surviving parent into one of their own homes without ever finding out if that is what the surviving parent wants. Still in shock over the loss, many elderly allow the children to do what appears to be best. This move, however, can be very devastating and cause serious problems of loneliness.

A widow of twenty-six years interviewed for the research project provided insight concerning solitude and being comfortable living alone. She was secure in living by herself and related in no uncertain terms that she never gets lonely. She had far too much to do ever to feel lonely. She had a lot of friends and acquaintances and probably corresponded with more people each week than most other people do at Christmas. Over the years, she has fought her children's attempts to get her to sell her home and move to an apartment near one of them, in a city far from her roots. Now all of her friends live close by; she has lived in this same town for over sixty years, and her husband is buried there. Leaving would be traumatic. She is comfortable in her big old family home, close to her lifelong friends, with her cat, all of her projects, and her memories.

During the early stages of the loneliness research, interviews were conducted with the elderly in Weeping Water, Nebraska, a small, quiet, rural town in the southeast corner of the state. Known as the Limestone Center of the World, it always seems a little dusty and desolate because of all the limestone quarries there. In one of the interviews a 72-year-old widow who was living alone in her two-story family home located on the edge of the town said: "You people up there in that big university think we old people are lonely, don't you? Well I want you to know that we are not. I have a daughter who is married to a fine young man, and I have two wonderful grandchildren. They visit me a lot on Sundays, and we have dinner together. I really enjoy them and especially my grandchildren. But I breathe a sigh of relief when that station wagon backs out of the driveway on Sunday afternoon and I can get back to doing the things I enjoy doing at this time in my life." She had a house full of plants and flowers. She worked in her garden and was active in her church and women's groups. She was a well-adjusted person who spoke for a large segment of the elderly.

Contact with kin does not always reduce loneliness and increase psychological well-being, while peer contact often does. Friendships offer benefits that kin relationships may not, including assistance, sharing of problems, and information. Being able to talk to someone who has been through similar experiences is helpful at any time in life, but particularly during large-scale and often traumatic changes, such as retirement, physical problems such as declining health, death of a spouse, and related changes in social interactions.

Intimacy is an important and often overlooked need and part of life for older adults. It has been found that the availability of a confidant was the strongest predictor of well-being in later adult life. For elderly people who are married, their spouse is often their confidant. Another particularly important factor in the life of an older adult is the feeling of predictability and control over one's environment. This feeling or perception becomes critical to general well-being. Many older adults who suffer physical disabilities find that their lives are taken over by their children. Often changes are made without consulting the parent, such as selling the house and car, moving the parent to a nursing home, and so on.

These types of changes limit mobility, remove the person from friends, and remove all control over life by reversing roles with one's children and forcing dependence. The elderly resist the invitation to move in with children because of this need for independence, privacy, and control.

It appears that once a person begins the struggle for independence as a child, the struggle never ceases. Adolescents push for it. Adults strive for a balance between dependence on a mate and independence that brings friends, interests, and activities separate from the spouse's. Elderly adults strive to not become dependent on their children.

Perception of control in one's life may be important in understanding why peer contact is better for the morale of an older person than contact with family members. We choose our friends; our family is determined for us. We have more control in friendships than with family relationships. This is especially true for the elderly, who may be ill or disabled. Friends are more likely to allow reciprocation for favors granted, be experiencing similar problems and thus be willing to discuss them, and probably are more readily available than families who have busy lives of their own.

## Factors Influencing Loneliness

When the study of the level of loneliness the elderly experience was started, it was expected that the elderly would be the loneliest group. This is the popularly held notion in our society. An elderly person's level of loneliness is one facet of the many stereotypes built around aging. But the research has shown that this notion is not true. Instead, the elderly as a group rated the least lonely. This finding lends substance to the more recent belief that loneliness is not a natural part of the aging process; it does not necessarily increase with advancing age. Certainly there are many lonely elderly people, just as there are in any other age group. Overall, however, the elderly, with their lifetime of experience, appear to have more realistic expectations. They are better adjusted to their current life situation than any of the other age groups.

The first research project concerned with the elderly and the levels of loneliness that they experience was completed by Harriette Woodward. This project, entitled "Loneliness among the Elderly," studied a representative sample of elderly people and the factors involved in their experiences with loneliness. Three hundred ninety people over 60 years of age, living in both urban and rural areas, participated in this study. All of the subjects completed the Loneliness Inventory during personal interviews.

The results of this study indicated that as a group, these older people were not extremely lonely. They were relatively well adjusted and accepting of their situation. Eight factors in the lives of these elderly people were found to contribute significantly to the loneliness they experience: gender, past occupation, happiness with housing situation, confinement, income range, state of health, feelings about retirement, and feeling of being loved and cared for.

Elderly women were lonelier than the men, a finding that does not differ from other studies on loneliness and gender. One of the factors that was not controlled in this study was widowhood. That a greater percentage of women than men in this study were widowed may have contributed to these findings. The widows in Karen Hornung's research, however, were not significantly lonelier than the women in this study, lending validity to the finding that women are lonelier than men. Woodward believed that another reason for the difference was that men are socially freer to sit and talk with old cronies and engage in impromptu social activities than are women, so the level of outside contact for elderly females is probably lower than that for males.

The influence of a person's past occupation was an interesting factor. Those who had worked as semiskilled laborers (taxidriver, machine tender, delivery person, laborer, and so on) were the loneliest. The housewife was the second loneliest of the occupational groupings. And individuals in the skilled category (carpenters, electricians, machinists) were the least lonely.

Whether the individual lived in an apartment, a housing complex, someone else's home, or his or her own home was not found to be a factor contributing to loneliness scores. Also not important was the urban or rural location of the residence. Feelings about the living arrangements, however, did influence loneliness scores. The majority of the people in this study indicated that they were happy where they lived. These people had significantly lower loneliness scores than those who said that they were unhappy. The elderly who indicated unhappiness with their housing situation, perhaps because they felt confined to their home, may have been frustrated that they could not change their situation. They were lonely through circumstances beyond their control. These findings emphasize that the most important aspects of housing for senior citizens are that they are comfortable, feel safe, and, most of all, are content with their living arrangements.

Income amounts influenced loneliness scores. Those in the lowest income groups had the highest loneliness scores, and the least lonely were in the middle range. Feelings about adequacy of income did not prove to be a significant factor. It was no surprise, however, that those who said they "can afford everything" were less lonely than those who said their income was "not adequate at all." Another interesting finding was that as income increased above the middle range, loneliness scores increased also.

An individual's belief about his or her level of health was found to be related to loneliness score. Participants who perceived their health as being excellent or good experienced less loneliness than did those who said their health was average or poor.

Loneliness scores for the elderly still employed and those retired did not differ significantly. Feelings about retirement, not whether one was retired, influenced loneliness scores.

Those who found that retirement was not all they had expected it to be were lonelier than those who felt it was all they had anticipated. Feelings of being let down can contribute to loneliness.

The final factor found to influence loneliness in the elderly was the feeling of being loved and cared for. Those who felt they were "almost always" loved and cared for were significantly less lonely than those who felt "often" or "sometimes" loved and cared for. No one in this study responded that they were "rarely" or "never loved and cared for."

Of interest too are some of the variables studied that were found not to be related to feelings of loneliness. There was no difference in loneliness for subjects whose children lived just blocks away or miles away. Although elderly who "rarely" or "never" saw their children were somewhat lonelier than the "sometimes" and "often" groups, it was not a significant amount. There was no real difference in loneliness scores for those who said they had a meaningful church association and those who said they did not. The meaningfully related group, however, did have slightly higher loneliness scores.

## Homes for the Elderly

Using the result of Woodward's study, Marcia Wythers took the study of the elderly one step further and researched a specific segment of the elderly population: residents in homes designated for the elderly. There were 145 participants in this study over the age of 60 living in elderly housing facilities in a midwestern city. They completed the Loneliness Inventory during an interview with a researcher.

This group was found not to be particularly lonely, but they were somewhat lonelier than their peers still living in their own homes. The following factors were significantly related to loneliness: gender, marital status, health, feelings about the past year, discontentment, introversion, and a recent move to a new location. Only two factors, gender and health of the subject, used in the previous research project were examined in this study, and they were again found to influence the loneliness levels of elderly people.

Women were again found to be lonelier than men. Widowed, divorced, and never-married elderly individuals were lonelier than married individuals. Those in poor health were lonelier than those in good or excellent health. Attitude plays a large part in loneliness as shown through the influence of the following factors: those who felt that the past year had been "very happy" or "happy" were less lonely than those who felt it had been "unhappy" or "neither happy nor unhappy," and those who were discontent were lonelier than those who were not. Introverted individuals were lonelier than those who were not. Individuals who thought of themselves as "shy" were lonelier than those who said they were not shy. The elderly who had lived in their present living arrangement one year or less were lonelier than those who had lived there four to nine years.

There were no differences or relationships with loneliness for the following variables: age, 60 to 90 and over; whether they had children; handicapped or not handicapped; frequency of church attendance; whether they had a hobby; and amount of time spent alone.

## Widows

"How long has it been since someone touched me? Twenty years? Twenty years I've been a widow," writes Donna Swanson in her powerful poem, "Minnie Remembers." How many 20-year-old women who marry a 22-year-old man expect to outlive their groom by an average of more than eight years? According to the Institute of Life Insurance, many women are widows for much longer than eight years, and for women in general, the average is fifteen to twenty-five years of widowhood.

Almost all older married women will experience widowhood. One-half of all women in American society are widowed by age 65, says author Robert Butler. According to recent census statistics, elderly women are more likely to be widowed than married. In 1988, the average age of widowhood in the United States was 56. Further, 12.5 percent of the female population in the United States is widowed and most of them live in metropolitan areas.

Since there are more than five and one-half times as many widows as widowers, and two of every five elderly women live alone, research into the extent of loneliness in the elderly is crucial. The lives of older urban widows can be better understood by determining the extent of their loneliness, how and when they experience this loneliness, and the social and demographic variables that contribute to their loneliness.

Karen Hornung conducted a study that addressed the problem of loneliness among urban widows. Her research found that several social and demographic variables significantly influenced the extent of loneliness an elderly urban widow experienced: length of marriage, length of widowhood, satisfaction with amount of organizational activity, and feelings about the past year.

Older urban widows who had been married fifty years or more at the time of the death of their spouse were the loneliest group. They were significantly lonelier than those who had been married thirty to thirty-nine years. Women who had been widowed five years or fewer were found to be significantly lonelier than women widowed more than five years. This finding supports much of the current research on bereavement, which has found that adjustment after the death of a spouse takes between two and five years.

Although widows who participated in a greater number of organizational activities (membership in clubs, groups, and senior centers) had higher loneliness scores, the relationship was not significant. The satisfaction with the amount of this type of activity was a contributing factor to loneliness. Those who felt that they did not participate as much as they wanted were significantly lonelier than those who felt that they did. The important factor here was not the amount of activity but the satisfaction with it.

Happiness proved to be another important factor in relation to loneliness. Older urban widows who felt "happy" about the past year were not as lonely as those who felt that the past year had been either "satisfactory" or "unhappy." Those who responded that their last year had been "satisfactory" were significantly less lonely than those who were "unhappy." As with many other circumstances in life as shown in earlier research results, our perception of the situation can affect our feelings about it much more than the actual situation does.

Some findings were particularly interesting because they were not found to be significantly related to degree of loneliness: age (60–85 and over); education (fourth grade to graduate or professional education); whether they lived alone; frequency of telephone use; visiting patterns of relatives and of freinds ("as often as I want" to "not nearly as often as I want"); whether they felt confined to their home; and time spent alone each day.

## Retirement

It is deplorable that until a few years ago, the compulsory retirement age was 65. It was said that mandatory retirement was the only answer to the problem of the aging worker. Even now, the age has been raised only to age 70 in most situations. Many people are not against retirement; they only wish that they could afford to retire. The point is that individuals should be able to retire when they are ready and not when somebody else wants them to. Part of being ready to retire may include the fact that the worker can no longer do the job. The problem here is determining when that point is. This does not seem like a real or a legitimate concern; this issue is faced and resolved every day in businesses, and age is not even a factor. Moreover, the list of famous people who made tremendous contributions long past "normal" retirement age is legion: Theodor Seuss Geisel ("Dr. Seuss"), Winston Churchill, Carl Sandburg, Robert Frost, Frank Lloyd Wright, Matisse, Michelangelo, Thomas A. Edison, and Sigmund Freud, to name a few.

At a recent seminar on loneliness and the elderly, several retired businessmen lamented the fact that on the day before their retirement, everyone still sought their time and opinions, and the day after retirement, no one was interested. This is true much too often in our society. Some more enlightened businesses take advantage of the expertise of the people who are retiring and retain them as consultants. The time they spend consulting with the company may be only a few hours a week or month, and the pay cannot interfere with retirement benefits (that is, they can't make more than social security allows before losing some benefits). But the pay is not important; what is important is the benefit to the company and the retiree.

Volunteer situations can be of great benefit too. A rehabilitation counselor who retired almost twenty years ago volunteers at a retirement rehabilitation center for several hours each day. Rehabilitation was her life before retirement, and now it continues to give her life and something to look forward to each day.

Another person was forced into early disability retirement at age 55 because he was going blind. He was in a management position, and his job required travel. He became a volunteer management consultant for the Small Business Administration. He said, "It is so much fun sharing your knowledge with young people who don't know the first thing about business." He added, "You know, I sit behind a big desk answering all their questions, and they don't even know that I am blind."

## Coping Strategies

Well, are they "golden years" or "tarnished brass"? For many of the elderly, these are hard years. Illness, poverty, forced retirement, death of loved ones, abandonment, infirmities of old age, and abject loneliness haunt them. But there are ways to survive loneliness and to make life more meaningful and fulfilling at this stage in life.

The prescription seems to be the one miracle drug that works for any situation: acceptance. The elderly have to be accepting of this stage in life; they have to admit that they are old. This seems to be tough to do before 70, but it needs to be done much earlier. After accepting this stage of their lives, they must proceed to take advantage of it and develop a positive attitude. After all, it took them a long time to get there. The elderly can use the wisdom that can be acquired only from age and experience.

Research indicates that the years past 60 should be as golden as any other. There are problems, but there are problems at every other stage of the life cycle. No one ever said it would be easy, but it doesn't need to be dismal. Each of us is the key to making our life what we want it to be. Certainly we can seek the help and counsel of others, but only we can make the difference. Youth is not wasted on the young, and the wisdom of old age should not be wasted by the elderly.

# 6

# Factors Associated with Loneliness

IT becomes obvious from the research that some factors are commonly associated with loneliness at all stages of the life cycle. This chapter will identify these factors and examine them and the relationship to loneliness.

## Gender

One of the common determiners of the degree of loneliness in most periods of life is gender. In all of the studies, it was found that females were lonelier than males, or there was no difference. In an attempt to explain this finding, we reexamined the Loneliness Inventory to determine whether it could be biased toward one sex. But the examination by experts in the field of psychology and a statistical procedure convinced us that the instrument is not sexually biased. In other words, the responses to the questions are not gender dependent.

Are women truly lonelier than men, or is it just culturally more acceptable for women to express weakness than it is for men? The Loneliness Inventory is a self-reporting instrument. In our society, and in many others, loneliness tends to be viewed as a weakness. Is it socially acceptable for men to express a weakness such as loneliness? Such a self-disclosure might be viewed more negatively for men than it would be for women. Perhaps men are not willing to admit, even to themselves, that they could be as lonely as women. Beginning in childhood, society allows little girls to express their emotions and weakness far more than little boys. When little girls fall and skin themselves, we probably say something like, "I know it hurts. Go ahead and cry. Let me kiss it and make it all better." In the same situation with our little boys, we would probably say, "It's just a little scratch. Come on now; big boys don't cry." Even as adults the "big boys don't cry" admonition prevails. Men are not permitted by social custom to be emotional in public. About the only time it is socially acceptable for a man to cry in public is in times of extreme grief; the loss of a ball game isn't enough.

Women may cry in public or almost anywhere else for almost any reason. Women are "allowed" to show their emotions whether they are miserable or euphoric, unhappy or happy. They cry at weddings, funerals, graduation, movies, birthday parties, when parting, when reuniting, and whether they win or lose the game. Our culture is starting to encourage men to show emotion, but even now most real men wouldn't be caught dead crying or even being too euphoric at being crowned, say, homecoming king. Not only do women cry to express their happiness on these occasions; almost everyone has come to expect and accept this response.

Another explanation for the finding that women are lonelier than men is that compared to men, women are more emotional. They are probably much more in touch with their feelings and emotions than are men. It is generally felt that women consider interpersonal relationships more important than do men. Women who feel that they have deficiencies in this area are certainly more concerned about it than men are. In the studies reported here, women more than men were less lonely if they felt "loved and cared for," had someone with whom to share responsibility and decision making, had friends and relatives to telephone, had a confidant, and had high marital satisfaction. Although these were important to men also, they were found to be significantly more important to women.

## Transportation

Transportation availability was another important factor related to feelings of loneliness. Those who had adequate transportation were less lonely than those who did not. Reasons for this finding seem obvious in a society constantly on the move. If you cannot go where you want to when you want to, you are probably going to feel frustrated and lonely. Inability to have the freedom of movement provided for by ready transportation causes most people to feel isolated and lonely.

Modern society depends on the automobile. No other invention has had so great an impact on our way of life. Its development gave a freedom of movement not possible before. It also created a whole new expectancy in people and in our way of doing things. The arrival of the drive-in didn't stop with root beer stands. Now there are drive-in banks, movies, laundries, dry cleaners, liquor stores, tax consultants, churches, and even funeral homes. How can anyone help but feel alienated, isolated, and lonely in a society so dependent on the car if one is not available?

## Self-Esteem

Self-esteem is commonly associated with loneliness. It was not measured in all of the studies, but when it was, its relationship to loneliness was clear. Individuals with low self-esteem were the loneliest, no matter what other factors were present.

## Ease in Making Friends

Ease in making friends was found to be common to the studies. The ability to form intimate interpersonal relationships is very closely related to self-esteem. Those who lack favorable self-esteem cannot expect to attract the interest of others. Individuals who found it easy to make friends were the least lonely.

## Happiness

With the exception of the alcoholic subjects, feelings of happiness during the past year was another factor common to all the projects. The happier the subjects said they had been during the past year, the less lonely they were. This is not an unexpected finding, but it does point out that lonely people are not very happy. Happiness then becomes an important factor to consider in combating loneliness.

Happiness during the past year is closely related to another factor found commonly related to loneliness: closeness of family relationships. The closer the individual perceives the relationships with family, the less lonely they are. This finding strikes at the heart of the definition of loneliness and the need for significant interpersonal relationships. The primary support group for most of us is the family. The term *family* can be ambiguous because a lot of people use the term indiscriminately to describe all kinds of social groups. In the loneliness research, the term *family* referred to the nuclear family. This family usually consists of a mother and father and at least one offspring. The research demonstrated that closness to family is an important determiner of degree of loneliness.

## Money

Money is related to loneliness. The amount of money a person has is not the important factor; it is the perception of the adequacy of this money that makes the difference. The degree to which a person feels he or she has enough money for needs and wants determines the intensity of loneliness. When lack of finances limits activity, feelings of helplessness and loneliness may arise. The fact that money is associated with status in our society cannot be ignored. A lack of it may depreciate status and self-esteem, which again leads to loneliness.

## Days and Seasons

The seasons found to be lonely vary. For many, there was no one loneliest season. For college students, both summer and winter were lonely. Summer was lonely because they missed the friendships made during the school year. In the summer, friends scatter; they go home, go to summer school, get a job. In the winter, the college students missed family when they returned to college. Divorced subjects said that spring was lonely because "spring is the time you are supposed to be paired with someone." Because the studies were conducted in Nebraska, winter was a lonely time. It is not only cold and dreary; it is confining. For many people, especially the elderly, they practically become shut-ins.

Most of the people in the studies did not designate any one particular day of the week as the loneliest. For a large percentage, however, Sunday was considered the loneliest. Although there were some differences among the research groups, Saturday was the next choice. Weekends appear to be lonely times, probably because everyone looks forward to them so much. For some, the weekend is a time to get out of the rat race and enjoy the peace that comes from aloneness. It is also a time to be with loved ones. But for the largest percentage of our subjects, it was a lonelier time. A regional vice-president of a large insurance company, who is a very positive person, has a somewhat different attitude. His motto is, "Thank God it's Monday so I can get on with what I love to do with the people I love to do it with." When he says this at office meetings, there are a lot of groans; however, a large number of people are honestly glad to be back at work on Monday mornings. Work may be their only social contact. Without their occupation, they are very lonely people.

## Age Relationships

Is loneliness age related? The research would tend to say that it is. Preschool children are on the low end of the continuum of loneliness, as are the elderly. Adolescents as a group are the loneliest, except for individuals who are in a crisis situation such as alcoholism. Even here, the younger adolescents are the loneliest. This suggests that loneliness follows a curvilinear pattern, increasing with age up through adolescence and then gradually decreasing except in times of stress or crisis, such as alcoholism, divorce, illness, bereavement, or economic hardship. Not only unhappy events cause problems with loneliness. Happy events such as graduation, going away to college, engagements, weddings, a new job, and moving to a new home are considered positive happenings, but they can still cause stress and crisis that may lead to loneliness.

## Unrelated Factors

Some factors did not seem to make any difference as far as loneliness was concerned. The findings concerning religion and loneliness are probably the most interesting, and perhaps the most controversial. In all the studies, it was found that church (religious service) attendance was not related to loneliness. One might speculate that the more frequently one attended religious services, the less lonely one would be. But these findings are quite conclusive. In fact, there is some evidence that those who never attended church were the least lonely.

After much debate and discussion with religious leaders, we concluded that we probably had measured the wrong factor. Church attendance may be an indication of religiosity, but it does not necessarily measure involvement. Just because a subject attended church every week did not mean that he or she was involved (except perhaps physically). One Christian minister said, "Unless you really accept the love of Jesus Christ and establish a personal relationship with Him, you could live in church and still be lonely." Other religious leaders agreed that acceptance and involvement, not mere attendance, are the important factors.

Another possible explanation for the finding may be one of population selectivity. Perhaps those who go to church are somewhat lonelier than those who do not. They are there because they are looking for help with their loneliness.

In addition it was found that there was no difference in loneliness among the various recognized religious faiths. This is not too difficult to understand; all are organized around certain religious doctrines and provide a place where people can worship together. What is more puzzling, is the finding that those who practiced no religious faith at all were the least lonely. Maybe since they are the least lonely, they do not feel a need for this kind of relationship and thus do not participate in religious organizations.

It might seem obvious that if individuals who found it easy to make friends were less lonely, the more close friends one had, the less lonely one would be. The number of close friends, however, was not related to how lonely individuals felt. Certainly those who made friends easily had close friends, but whether they had one or five did not make any difference. It is also true that some of the lonely people had close friends. How many close friends do you need to keep you from being lonely? One good close friend will do; the number is not important. It is how easily you make friends that counts. Clearly those with high self-confidence do not have to worry about how many close friends they have. Those who feel that they need friends are secure in the knowledge that they have the ability to attract them.

The number of activities in which the individuals participated was another factor commonly associated with loneliness. For adolescents, those involved in three to five extracurricular activities were lonelier than those involved in only one. For college students, the number of extracurricular activities was not significantly related to loneliness, but those with three to five activities had higher loneliness scores than those with fewer activities. For housewives, there was no significant relationship between the number of social activities and loneliness. There was a trend, however, for those with more activities to be lonelier.

A follow-up of these findings revealed reasons similar to those for religious participation. Those who participated in only a few activities were deeply involved in them; they were not just joiners. People who were trying to participate in a larger number of activities were still searching. In addition they had spread themselves so thin that they could not participate deeply in any of them.

In summary, the factors that were found to be commonly associated with loneliness at most stages of life were gender, transportation, self-esteem, ease in making friends, happiness, day of the week and season of the year, money, and age. Factors found not related to loneliness at all stages of the life cycle were religion, number of close friends, and number of activities.

# 7

# Pets and Loneliness

RECENTLY we have become aware of the importance of pets in our lives and to our well-being. We are just beginning to appreciate fully the effect they have on our existence. We can find books on the care and feeding of pets, human interest stories, and novels of the Lassie-come-home variety. Many films and television series have been made about the relationship of dogs and people. Over half of American homes—in fact, about 60 percent—have dogs as pets, and many have more than one.

Although dogs, cats, and other pets play an important part in our lives, there is little in the professional scientific literature concerning their importance in relieving feelings of loneliness. Yet pets have been part of human survival and escape from loneliness and solitude since the beginnings of recorded history. Some believe that the history of the development of humans cannot be separated from the development of their pets, especially dogs and cats.

Dogs have been "man's best friend" for thousands of years. This is one relationship that has survived the test of time—all time. Even the Bible has many references to pets, another indication of their importance in the development of civilization. The tomb of Amten in Egypt contains pictures of dogs in hunting scenes, dating dogs as pets and hunting partners of man between 3500 and 4000 B.C.

There is a saying among dog owners that there are only two

kinds of people in the world: those who have a dog and those who would like to have a dog. Although some people claim they do not like pets, very few are not moved by the loving and trusting look of a puppy or kitten.

The most common pets are dogs, cats, birds (parakeets and canaries), fish, guinea pigs, rabbits, and hamsters. People living in rural areas sometimes have larger animals as pets, including horses, sheep, goats, and even pigs. And some individuals have unusual or exotic pets—mice, snakes, skunks, raccoons, monkeys, and alligators—but the number is small compared to the dog and cat population.

Why we have pets in the first place may be somewhat of a mystery. They can be expensive and except for the more passive ones, such as goldfish, they can be demanding of time, energy, and money. Americans spend billions of dollars every year on the care and feeding of their pets. And there are beauty parlors, pet psychologists, schools, vacation kennels, and even summer vacation camps for dogs.

Although there are probably several plausible explanations as to why we keep pets, the one given most frequently is for companionship. It has been said also that pets may make a social statement about the individual. For example, you would not expect a macho man to choose a chihuahua over a pit bull terrier as a symbol of masculinity. And it is probably more of a status symbol to own a Great Pyrenees than a mutt. Moreover, as in the case of the automobile, home, clothes, and college attended, pets may be thought of as an extension of the individual's personality.

The definition of loneliness that has guided the Nebraska loneliness research and the coping strategies for dealing with loneliness states that loneliness is a feeling of being alone and disconnected or alienated from positive persons, places, or things. A pet may not be a person, place or thing, but pets have an important place in our hearts. They have been the cause of grief and loneliness when they are ill, die, are lost, or have to be given up, as well as great help in times of their owner's grief and loneliness. We do know that humans can be just as lonely for a pet as for a person. Human relationships are without question the most important for relieving feelings of loneliness, but they are not the only relationships that can help overcome our loneliness.

The theory and the research findings indicate that in the caring for others, in feeling needed, and in the giving of ourselves, we are able to get outside our own problems and feel less lonely. Pets require attention and care. They are unable to take care of themselves and appreciate everything done for them. Although some pets, such as fish, turtles, and lizards, are unable to express this appreciation in a demonstrable way, we are aware that without our care, they would not survive, and that understanding makes all the difference.

Pets are resilient to rejection and even abuse. When their masters are upset and treat them badly, they never ever ask, "Why me?" but instead act as if they have done something to make their master upset. They are willing to take the blame even when they are blameless.

Most of the vertebrates express appreciation and love by their demonstrable behavior and devotion to their masters. But even fish rush to the top of the tank when food is sprinkled on top of the water, and birds give out with a cheerful song when fed. Chickens run to the call of their provider, and the pigeons in public parks flock to the people who feed them.

## Young Children

Since there is no question about the value society places on animals, it becomes the family's responsibility to instill respect for and appreciation of animals in children. Pets are important to young children. They teach them love and devotion because pets give unconditional love, loyalty, and devotion to the child. Parents and other care givers may not always give unconditional love. They may say, in words or actions, "You do this or that, and I will love you." Or "You wouldn't do that if you really loved me." Not so with pets. A pet's love and devotion is given freely and unconditionally.

Pets can be important to the development of the child. They are dependent friends, thus encouraging a sense of responsibility, competence, self-esteem, and trust in the child. This may be especially important for children without siblings. They can get close to and love a pet.

Loss of a pet through death may be the child's first experience with death and bereavement. It thus provides the child with experience in dealing with the reality of illness and death. They learn that death is not reversible. Parents need to help the young child through the grief process; they should not try to play down or minimize the loss. The child's grief is real, no matter how insignificant the parent may think the loss is. There is strong evidence that the death of a pet is a heartfelt experience for the impressionable child and must be met with great compassion.

Although it is probably a good plan to replace the pet within a reasonable length of time, the child should be given appropriate time to grieve before a new pet arrives. To introduce a new pet too soon might be giving the child the message that life is replaceable, and that when something dies, you can go out and get another one. They may also get the impression that the loss was not important to the parent. Thus, the death of a pet can be an opportune time for teaching the child the importance and value of life, as well as its finite properties.

Children respond to animals in almost every situation. It has been reported that the blood pressure of children placed in mildly stressful situations can be reduced by having an animal, such as a dog, present. Children apparently find situations less threatening when a pet is with them. Other research indicates the young children in families with pets are less lonely. Another study found that asthmatic children improved dramatically when their parents presented them with chihuahua dogs. It was hypothesized that these children now had something to think about besides their own illness. They had something that needed their care and love.

Children who have difficulty talking with other children and adults have few problems talking to pets. This can lead to better communication with parents and other children. Some children, not just those with communication problems, communicate with adults through their pets by talking to their pets in the presence of adults. The child might say, "Oscar, I sure wish I had a friend as good as you. I don't know why I have to eat all my cereal every morning; it makes my stomach hurt" or "I wish Daddy wouldn't yell at Mommy so much." In this way, the child can get some very powerful messages heard without fear of rejection by the adult. The parents can also use this means of communicating with the child: "Oscar, it is time to go to bed now, so you better pick up your toys and get ready." By talking to the pet in the presence of the child, the message may be more acceptable and less threatening to the child. The result could be better relationships with the child, especially one with difficulty communicating. This gives the child positive experiences on which to build relationships.

## Adolescents and Young Adults

In a recent study of adolescents and loneliness, it was found that adolescents who had pets, such as dogs, cats, or horses, were significantly less lonely than those who did not have pets. These adolescents said that when they were lonely and depressed, their pets seemed to sense their problem and gave them more attention and stayed by them. They said that this companionship made them feel less lonely.

One teenage girl said, "At least I can depend on my faithful dog Blacky. He knows and understands when I am blue and lonely and listens to me without talking back. He gives me something to live for and care for." Another high school student said, "When I feel real down and lonely coming home from school to an empty house, I know that old Chips will be there to greet me with his whole body wagging because he is so glad to see me. I may have had a bummer of a day, but he makes all the difference. The first thing I know, I am talking and laughing, and we have an after-school snack together. He brings me out of my loneliness, and I can get on with my homework with a better attitude toward the whole world. When my mother comes home, she always asks me if Chips has been helping me with my homework, and I always say yes because he always does."

Young adults living alone find their pets important to them. One young man who works for an insurance company said that his cocker spaniel is the best thing that ever happened to him. He cannot go home every day at noon to let the dog out, so he leaves the patio door slightly open. He said, "I know that it costs a lot of money when it is bitter cold outside, but he is worth every penny of the additional heating bill."

Another young person said that if it had not been for her cat, she would probably have ended up with some serious personal problems. She had moved to a city because there were no jobs in the small town where she grew up. She knew no one in the city and lived alone, and was lonely. She missed her parents and her high school friends. Because she could not bear going home to an empty apartment after work, she started going straight from work to a bar, where she spent the evening. She would then go home, go to bed, get up the next morning, go to work, and repeat the process. She realized that she was having a problem when her supervisor talked to her about the decline in her work. He told her that it was not only her work that he was worried about but that her relationships with her coworkers were also deteriorating. In addition he said that he was concerned that she was on the verge of having a problem with alcohol and suggested that she talk with the company's psychologist.

The psychologist told her that she needed to break the destructive living pattern she had fallen into. Among other things, he told her that she needed something to go home to after work. He suggested that she get a significant pet, such as a dog or cat, to care for and to be there when she got home. She chose a cat because they are easier to have in an apartment. The cat made a real difference in her life. She now looks forward to going home after work because she knows that Tabby, her cat, is expecting her and needs her. Love begets love. She has a conversation ice breaker and stories to share with other pet owners at work. Her relationships with her supervisor and coworkers have improved dramatically, and so has her work. Although the cat was not the only factor in the successful turnaround of her self-destructive behavior pattern, it was an important element.

Pets do not care whether you are rich or poor, white or black, smart or dull, beautiful or ugly; they love you no matter what. One teenager said that sometimes when she is depressed and so lonely that she could die, she has a tendency to take out her feelings on her family and friends: "I snap at them, and they snap back. But my faithful cocker sort of stands back, looks at me with his big brown soulful eyes, and I can't help but smile at him. The minute I do, he is on my lap in a minute, kissing me all over. How can you stay in a bad mood when you have such a nonjudgmental, happy friend to get you out of it?" She added, "My parents could learn a lot about helping me from my dog."

## The Middle Years

Pets are an important part of the lives of those in the middle years of life too. According to some of the research in this area, people at this stage in life who have pets are much more compassionate toward others and are more satisfied and happier with their lives than are those without pets. This does not necessarily mean that there is a causal effect relationship between pet ownership and these factors, but they are related. Perhaps happy people are just more likely to have pets. Most of the pet owners in this age group report that they receive more companionship from their pets than from their friends.

Individuals in the middle years report that their dogs and cats provide them with companionship, are good for their health by helping them relax, offer protection, and provide them with a source of nonjudgmental acceptance, love, and loyalty. They also said that the pet gave them something to love and nurture, as well as a chance for uninhibited play.

One mother of four said that she would live a lonely life during the school year if it were not for the family's two cats and dog. She reported that the house seems empty on Monday mornings when the children go to school and her husband goes to work. But, she said, "The dog is always at my side as I go about my work in the house, and the cats are always nearby. I am not alone even when I stop long enough for a cup of coffee. My old friends are there, keeping me from being lonely."

For childless adults, a pet allows them to express nurturing feelings. The care and concern the pet requires may even prepare some childless couples for later parenthood. Pets provide adults, as well as all the other groups, with a sense of being needed. Pets present an opportunity for all kinds of interaction with others. Many adults get involved in showing their pets at competitive shows or go to clubs and classes in the training and grooming of their pets. This recreational activity may be important in relieving them of their loneliness. Through these activities, they meet other people with similar interests and form special friendships.

In the second part of the midlife period, many parents face what has been termed the empty nest syndrome. The children have left home, and the parents are left alone in a house full of memories. This can be a lonely time for the parents. It may be especially lonely for women who have concentrated most of their time and attention for the past twenty-five years on their husband's career and their children. Some mothers wonder if there is anything to live for after the children leave.

Sometimes among things left behind when the children

depart are the pets. Although they cannot take the place of the children, they can be a great help during this transition time. One mother reported that she didn't know what she would have done without the family dogs; they seemed to understand how lonely she was and never left her side. They brought back and kept alive many memories of the time when the children were home. When her children call, their first questions are about how the dogs are. The family pets helped this woman during this transition period so that she could make decisions on what she wanted to do with the rest of her life.

## The Later Years

Many of the elderly said that their pets gave them something to get up for in the morning. One elderly woman said that her dog did not care that she was old and not beautiful anymore: "He still loves me and depends on me, and I depend on him. Since I got Checkers, I am not lonely anymore because I am needed, and that makes all the difference."

Time has a less important meaning for those who are retired, and they no longer have a rigid daily schedule. But pets make demands on their time and require them to maintain a daily routine. Their pets include birds, cats, dogs, fish, and, in one case, a goat. Many of the elderly living alone had numerous pets.

For the elderly living alone, whose children have grown and moved away, a pet gives them a chance to give and receive affection and to feel a renewed sense of personal worth. Sharing one's home with a pet is a sure way to overcome loneliness.

Many elderly say that a pet, especially a dog, gives them a sense of personal security. Some older people worry about security because their senses are no longer as sharp as they once were. They report that because of its keen senses of hearing and smell, their dog alerts them when there is someone at the door or anywhere around their house. Although the pet may not be a trained guard dog, potential intruders may go away when they know that someone has been alerted to their presence. Dogs also help their owners hear the telephone in various ways. Some report that their dogs come to get them when they hear the telephone even though they are not so trained. There are numerous reports of pets of all kinds alerting and saving their family from fires and other disasters.

Research has indicated that pets can be an important helping factor with health problems. One project demonstrated that when people with hypertension and high blood pressure who owned pets stroked their pet, their blood pressure was lowered. There was no change in their blood pressure when they stroked animals that did not belong to them. For a significant number of those who did not own pets, their blood pressure was lowered when they stroked any of the pets.

Having a dog around may help people in the later years with an exercise program. Exercise programs are important for all age groups but especially for the elderly. Walking is reportedly one of the most beneficial exercises and can be a pleasant experience when it is shared. Dogs are excellent walking companions and are insistent on the routine. One man's physician told him that he needed to walk at least a half-hour each day. He found walking around the neighborhood a lonely experience until he decided to take his dog. A beautiful dog—or any other dog, for that matter—is always an attraction to other people. This man now has a companion to share the walk and is stopped by people along the way who comment on his dog. Children who paid no attention to him before talk to him now because they are interested in the dog. He has made new friends through his dog and is usually gone on his walk twice as long as before.

Dogs keep their owners on their exercise program. We can all find excuses not to exercise, but dogs will not let us get away with this. They are so excited when it is time for their walk that their enthusiasm is contagious. Some dogs bring their leash to the owner when it is time for the walk. And they make you feel guilty if you even look as if you are not going to take them.

Many elderly have to give up their pets when they move into housing units or homes for the elderly. These homes are beginning to learn about the importance of pets to the welfare of their residents. Some designate one day of the week as pet day. If one of the residents had to give up a pet upon moving into the home, this may be the only way they can see their old friend. One elderly man said that he looks forward to this visit and added, "Sometimes I feel a little guilty because I am more excited about seeing my old dog than my family." One daughter said that her father calls her every day to see how his dog is getting along but does not seem too interested in the rest of the family. She said that she understood because her father's dog had been his constant companion for many years.

Some pet owner volunteer organizations in cities take their pets on visits to homes for the elderly and to rehabilitation centers on a regular basis. These volunteers report that their own rewards may be as great as the happiness they bring to residents. These weekly pet visits promote social, physical, and verbal interactions at these facilities. The residents love to pet the animals. It gives them something soft to hug and touch, and the animals respond enthusiastically. It also gives them an opportunity for social interactions with staff, volunteers, and other residents.

Animals are social facilitators. The presence of pets increases the sociability among all of the residents in the care facility. Pets become the topic of conversation, with discussion of their former pets, and sometimes the pets they had to give up when they moved into the care center. Often these discussions bring positive recollections, which include childhood memories of pets. They reminisce about family and tell stories that are associated with animals. When relatives visit on days other than pet day, the focus often is on pet day and how many memories it brought to mind.

Some homes for the elderly allow residents to have their

own pets. The argument against this arrangement has been that pets cause problems because they need care and attention. This is true to a certain extent, of course, but in the majority of cases, the residents who are able are more than happy to be responsible for the care of the pets and in turn do not require so much staff time for their own care. This activity gives them something to do and to think about. It takes them away from their own problems and loneliness, and they feel needed and loved.

A few states have laws that regulate against animals in homes for the elderly, and all have laws that govern food preparation and service in any public facility. These laws and regulations have been applied to homes for the elderly, but they pertain only to the food preparation and eating areas.

The loss of a pet, from death or some other reason, can cause acute grief in individuals of all ages, and especially in the elderly. The death of a pet can precipitate a grief as intense as the loss of a human, and sometimes even greater for the elderly. The pet is not only considered a family member; it may be the constant and only companion of an elderly person. For the elderly, the pet may play the role of a child. Like a child, the pet is given complete care; it is fed, cuddled, loved, and talked to. The pet's death may cause much disorganization in the life of its owner and his or her ability to function. Because the death of a pet is a significant event, the owner's friends and relatives need to be compassionate and understanding and talk about replacing the pet in time.

Recently the monkey of an 82-year-old organ grinder died after performing with the old man for over twenty-five years. At the funeral, there was but one mourner, the old man. The monkey was dressed in his little red suit and red cap and lying in a small casket. The old man told an interested bystander, "You may think this is all ridiculous, but he was all I had; he was my family, and I loved him very much." The old man said as the casket was lowered into the ground, "I will see you again soon old friend."

## Recommendations

Pets are important to people at all stages of development. Individuals can benefit from the companionship role animals play throughout life. The most signfiicant pets are considered to be dogs, cats, and horses, but there is evidence that other pets—birds, fish, guinea pigs, hamsters, and rabbits, for example—can have a significant impact on relieving feelings of loneliness.

Owning a pet has to be a personal decision, but to see the eyes of a child or an elderly person light up at the sight of a puppy or a kitten should be convincing enough. Parents must not make the mistake of depriving a child of the experience of having and loving an animal because it is not convenient. Most things in life that are important require work, and pets have been important to humans for centuries. A child deprived of a pet may be deprived of an important aspect of human development.

It is important to choose the right pet. With dogs, there is a wide selection of 121 different breeds and varieties of purebred dogs plus mixed breeds. A number of books on the breeds and their characteristics are available for helping in the selection. The American Kennel Club's *The Complete Dog Book* describes in detail the recognized purebred dogs. Local humane societies have dogs for adoption.

Prospective dog owners need to consider the purpose of getting a dog, where the dog will live, and even the personality of those for whom the dog is intended. Apartment dwellers should select a breed that will fit their living situation. For the elderly, a mature dog may be best because it will be house trained and not need as much full-time attention as a puppy.

A cat may be a good choice for apartment dwellers. Cats require less care, are much more independent than dogs, and can live totally inside. The choice of cats ranges from the very expensive and somewhat exotic varieties to so-called alley cats. Size is not usually a problem, but temperament may be.

Books, veterinarians, and friends who have cats can offer good advice.

Birds are successful as pets for all ages, especially for the elderly. They too require less care and bring great joy with their beauty and their song. Parakeets and parrots are the most popular talking birds. They can be trained to fly around the house when their cage is opened and then alight on their owner's shoulder. Fish aquariums have been used in homes for the elderly, as well as with individuals living alone, with great success. If caring for the aquarium is a problem, most pet stores offer a weekly service at low cost.

The important variable in all the studies and observations for how pets help people cope with their loneliness, as well as life in general, seems to be the selection of a suitable pet.

The relationship of humans and animals is as strange as it is wonderful. Friends may turn against you, and your sons and daughters prove ungrateful. Those whom you trusted most may become unworthy of your trust. When everything you have worked so hard for is gone and you are old and alone, the one that will stand by you, and lick your hand even though you have no food to give, and guard you zealously is your faithful companion dog.

# 8

# Living with Loneliness

THIS chapter is designed to help you cope with loneliness. There is no complete escape from loneliness. It is part of being born, of being human, of living, of loving, of dying. Perhaps there shouldn't be a complete escape. Why would anyone want to be deprived completely of an emotion? To experience the emotions of passion, happiness, grief, love and loneliness is part of living, part of being human.

But too much of anything is probably not a good thing. To be consumed by too much love can be as devastating as too much grief. There is some evidence that too much loneliness can cause physical illness and death. It can be destructive, but it can also be creative. The pain of loneliness, like physical pain, alerts us to the fact that something is not right in our lives, and in order to survive we need to do something about it. Loneliness reminds us that as humans, we need relationships, we need companionship, and we need others. To relieve this pain, we know that we must reach out to others. Without the pain of loneliness, we would remain unaware and miss the most important expression of our existence, relationships. The answer to surviving and going beyond loneliness is that we must establish and maintain human relationships.

## Rural Residents

The research completed concerning rural people and loneliness obtained information concerning how to prevent or cope with their feelings of loneliness. They were asked what resources they use, what available resources they do not use, what resources they would use if they were available, and what resources they would not use even if they were available. Under various headings there was a list of fifty-three resources, plus a place to list others after each category.

The following is a list of the resources available that were used more than 40 percent of the time by these adults:

Restaurants, 84 percent

Shopping centers or stores, 80 percent

A friend, 69 percent

Physician, 68 percent

Medical clinic, 68 percent

Hospital, 65 percent

Zoo or park, 50 percent

Clergy, 46 percent

Theater, 44 percent

Cooperative Extension Service, 43 percent

Lounge or bar, 41 percent

None of the following items was listed as being used 40 percent or more of the time: church group activities, social organizations and clubs, organized sports and recreation, individual sports and recreation, volunteer activities, adult education classes, public transportation, and miscellaneous resources.

If the resources listed as used more than 40 percent of the time were not available to some people, they were on their "would use" list. In addition to these resources, "community recreation centers" was also high on the "would use if available" list.

The rural adult subjects were asked to respond to forty-three "things" they did to prevent or cope with loneliness. They were also given an opportunity to add others. The following is a list of things men and women reported they did more than half the time to prevent or cope with loneliness: keep myself busy, 91 percent; read the newspaper, 67 percent; do garden or yard work, 61 percent; work overtime, 61 percent; pray, 56 percent; and activities with my spouse, 55 percent. Males were more likely to watch TV, 51 percent to 38 percent for females, and females cleaned house 53 percent to 20 percent for males.

The only item in the interpersonal relationships area used more than 50 percent of the time was "activities with my spouse." The percentages for other activities in this area were: telephone friends, 26 percent; telephone relatives, 34 percent; invite friends over, 17 percent; go visit friends, 18 percent; get out where there are other people, 34 percent; and do activities with your children, 36 percent. It is no wonder that these rural people have the highest lonely scores for adult groups. Not only have they fallen on hard times, but they have not utilized the basic methods for coping with their loneliness: interacting with others.

The adult subjects reported that they "never" or "rarely" did the following activities to relieve feelings of loneliness (this does not mean that they did not do these things; it just means they did not do them very often to relieve feelings of loneliness): participate in sports, 78 percent; write a letter, 50 percent; smoke/chew tobacco, 83 percent; to go to movies, 78 percent; use medication, 74 percent; drink alcoholic beverages, 75 percent; participate in social club activities, 65 percent; rearrange furniture, 64 percent; do volunteer work, 60 percent; read self-improvement books, 57 percent; read novels or fiction, 55 percent; or work out or exercise, 54 percent. This list shows that they did not engage much in destructive practices (for example, use drugs) to prevent or cope with loneliness, but it also shows that they failed to engage in positive practices.

Rural adolescents listed the following as the resources they used to cope with loneliness more than 40 percent of the time:

Clubs (4-H, Future Farmers of America, and so forth), 91 percent

Friends, 90 percent

Shopping centers/stores, 89 percent

Family, 88 percent

Swimming pool, 88 percent

Restaurants/fast food, 87 percent

Swimming/boating, 83 percent

Hiking/biking/skiing, 78 percent

Theaters/movies, 77 percent

Public library, 77 percent

Brother/sister, 75 percent

Music/musical instruments, 70 percent

Sunday school, 69 percent

Music (choir, band, orchestra, etc.), 66 percent

Teacher, 65 percent

Hospitals/medical clinics, 64 percent

Camping, 62 percent

Hunting/fishing, 61 percent

Bowling/billiards, 59 percent

Parks or zoos, 59 percent

Baseball/softball, 55 percent

Basketball, 55 percent

Bowling/roller skating, 54 percent

Physician, 47 percent

Church youth group, 46 percent

Volleyball, 42 percent

Crafts/needlework, 41 percent

The adolescents used the available resources a great deal more than the adults. As with the adults, when the resources used the most were not available, the adolescents wanted them. They wanted a youth center, which would provide a central gathering place and allow for increased interaction with peers.

To prevent or cope with loneliness more than 50 percent of the time, adolescents listed: keep myself busy, 75 percent; listen to music, 72 percent; watch TV, 69 percent; participate in sports, 55 percent; and play with pets, 55 percent.

It becomes quite clear why the rural adolescents are so lonely. In the top 50 percent of the things they do to prevent or cope with loneliness, they do not list one item that provides mainly for human interaction. Only sports comes close, and this may not always be considered a personal interaction item.

The adolescent group reported the following as things they did not do to prevent or cope with loneliness more than 50 percent of the time: use drugs, 99 percent; smoke/chew tobacco, 96 percent; drink alcoholic beverages, 95 percent; telephone relatives, 58 percent; and do volunteer work, 55 percent. At least they do not seem to be using negative coping methods.

## Loneliness or Solitude

There is a real difference between loneliness and solitude. The two can occur together, and sometimes do, but they are not contingent upon one another. You can be alone and not lonely or lonely and not alone. Solitude is something people choose for themselves. It can be a creative, intuitive, and productive experience. Yet most people in our society seem to fear it. Nevertheless, solitude may be necessary to help people keep their sanity. Nearly everyone needs to get away from the daily "circuit overload" once in awhile. It may only be a ten-minute coffee break, but it's important. Most individuals treasure periods alone so that they can have time to think without constant interruption.

Privacy and the opportunity for solitude need to be built into lives. In general people, especially teenagers, cherish the privacy of their own space. To share one's life is the most important way to overcome loneliness, but we also need "refueling" time. It is not always possible for everyone in a family to have his or her own room, but all family members should have a place where they can get away from other family members.

Although privacy is important, the home is also a place for emotional and social development. Making the children's rooms so attractive that they spend all their time there is not good. Neither the children's room nor the master bedroom should be so private that they are off-limits to other members of the family at all times.

Family rooms and recreation rooms should be the most attractive rooms in the house. Next in line should be the eating space, a place to draw the family together. It is important for the family to have at least one meal together every day, particularly during the teenage years. In our fast-paced society, it is not difficult to find excuses for not attending the dinner hour. But nothing should be allowed to interfere with this time for family interaction.

Being physically alone does not mean not feeling the presence of others. People can be hundreds of miles away from loved ones and still feel that they are not alone. "Even though we are far apart, our thoughts and prayers are with you" is not a meaningless statement.

Although we may not choose loneliness, it is not forced upon us any more than solitude; we only think it is. Loneliness is actually an affliction of the ego, a problem with the self. It is not so much concerned with our outside world as it is with our inside world. For example, consider people in similar situations, some will be lonely and some will not.

Adult children should not force their elderly parents to move into a retirement home because they think it is best for their health and well-being. The move might cause a significant problem, not the least of which is loneliness. Research in this area indicates that it is not where one lives or the conditions of that living that are important but one's attitude that makes the difference. Those who are unhappy with the arrangement will be lonely. The best and the worst health care centers for the elderly have residents who are lonely and those who are not lonely at all. Some older persons may be better off staying in their own homes, even if it shortens their lives by a few years. It is not the number of years we live that is important; it is the quality of those years that is vital.

Sometimes, no matter how much we would like to follow the wishes of our loved ones, we cannot do so. They may require the professional care of a home. The choice of a nursing home should be guided by several considerations. First and most important, if at all possible, the elderly person must be involved in the decision. There then needs to be an investigation of staff competency, the physical facility, the program, the patients, and the relationships between staff and residents. There are good nursing homes and bad ones. Sometimes there is not much of a choice because of the circumstances.

The financial resources to afford the care we would like may not be available. Nursing care for the elderly is expensive. Medicare pays for only a small part of the costs, which may range from $20,000 to $40,000 a year. With nursing home care, as with most anything else, you get what you pay for. Many older people start out in the more expensive homes. When all of their resources have been used up, they are forced to move into homes that operate almost totally on public assistance funds. Smaller communities may have only one facility, and it may be understaffed or staffed with individuals who are not well trained in the care of the elderly. The long-term care costs can easily impoverish the elderly as well as their children or others responsible for them.

After the nursing home has been chosen, the next step is to help the person who will reside there accept the situation. If he or she has been in on the decision from the start, this may not be a difficult task. If the elderly person is to be happy and not lonely, he or she must be accepting.

Consideration of a nursing home should start long before it is a critical or emergency situation. Some retirement homes provide transportation for anyone who wants to visit their facilities. They encourage potential residents to invite friends and children to learn about the program. Although their motivation may not be all altruistic, it is an opportunity to introduce the potential resident and the family to retirement care facilities.

Some people are lonely because they feel that they are inferior to everyone else. They mistakenly think that popular or beautiful people must be happier or more loved than they are. But these "beautiful" people suffer the same human frailties as everyone else. Because of their prominence or position, they may have many problems the "ordinary" person cannot imagine.

## Coping with Loneliness

There is no cure for loneliness. There are, however, ways to cope with loneliness, to put it off, to ease the pain, and to suffer it less frequently. The suggestions made here have helped many people combat loneliness. They may be considered prescriptions for easing the pain or for dealing with loneliness. They may or may not work for everyone, but they certainly won't work if they aren't tried.

First, lonely persons have to recognize and admit that they are lonely. There is nothing new in this. Before an alcoholic can benefit from treatment, he or she must acknowledge alcoholism. But few people will admit to being lonely. They say, "If I acknowledge being lonely, what I am saying in effect is that no one wants to be around me, to communicate with me, or to have any kind of relationship with me." It is a frightening thing to confess. Loneliness has to be recognized, however; the lonely person has to say, "I am lonely!"

Next, lonely people must take a good look at themselves. A care center chaplain in one of the loneliness research projects was puzzled over a situation with which he was dealing. A resident in the nursing home where he worked had little cause to be lonely, yet she complained bitterly and constantly about being "so terribly lonely." Although her husband had been dead for several years, most of her children and other family members lived close by. She was in relatively good health, and someone came to visit her every day. Most of the time she had several visitors each day. He said, "I don't know what to tell her." What he didn't understand was that this woman was milking her loneliness for all it was worth. She was probably afraid that if she told people she was not lonely, they would stop coming to see her. Loneliness is an attention-getter too. She needed to take a good look at herself. She may not have been aware that she was using her loneliness. Perhaps this woman enjoyed being lonely; some people seem to like to be miserable. Everyone needs to take a good look at themselves once in a while to make sure they are not using their loneliness in a negative way.

In order to relieve feelings of loneliness, we have to reach out to others. We have to be risk takers. If we are rejected, we must reach out again.

We must be honest with others. When we meet someone and

he or she says, "Hi. How's it going?" We must not reply "Fine!" if it's not. The person may not want to hear about all our troubles, or maybe they also need someone to talk with. A response might be, "I am really lonely today. I wish I just had somebody to talk to." Until we do this, people will not help us or we them. They might just say, "I'm a little down myself today. Let's talk." We should not take rejections personally. If the person says that he or she doesn't have time to talk, we can accept the statement as truth and reach out again. If we expect people to share their lives with us, it is necessary to share our life with them. Private people who never share anything with anyone else are probably very lonely people.

Sharing of one's self is important in work relations too. In the workplace, good supervisors take the time to get to know others, and to let others get to know them. Good supervisors know that when employees pass through the office door each morning, they don't leave their other life behind them, and neither do the supervisors. This attitude does not mean that they spend all their time socializing; it simply means that supervisors have to have respect for and show interest in their fellow workers and in the people they supervise.

When we go out socially, we should not expect too much. Adolescents have difficulty with this statement. For them, everything is intense and important, and they expect much. They should be told, "Don't expect to find Mr. Right or Ms. Perfect on the first date." If they expect this, chances are they will be disappointed. This expectation may seem ridiculous to some adults, but many lonely adults go out socially with the same hope. They are searching for the perfect person or the lasting relationship. We must be convinced instead that we can enjoy relationships that are less than perfect and are not necessarily deep and lasting.

Because loneliness is more involved with the inside world than the outside, we must look inward, not outward, for help with loneliness. We must depend on ourselves.

Research has confirmed what human development specialists have always known: the family is the most important institution. It is the one group that can't make you an "ex." You may have an ex-husband, ex-wife, ex-girl friend or ex-boss; but you never have an ex-family. No one has ever had an ex-daughter or ex-son. Regardless of family problems, we still belong to our family. If something is wrong within the family, we must try to straighten it out. Possibly we are part of the problem and therefore can become part of the solution. Family relationships are salvageable. Even in extreme situations, such as differences in moral values or life-styles, optimism is necessary. Some people may not think the effort is worthwhile, but it is. The research findings and counseling experience provide convincing evidence that families are helpful in coping with loneliness.

Individuals who have an outside interest that excites them and that they work at vigorously have fewer problems with loneliness. Outside interests need to be different from work. They provide an opportunity to meet people from different walks of life.

Joining organizations is a way to relieve feelings of loneliness, but just joining is not enough; we must become involved and participate by taking some responsibility. Even if we do no more than make the coffee for the meeting, that is better than doing nothing.

Friends are important. The research findings indicate that it is not the number of close friends that is important; it is the ability to make them that makes the difference. The quality or degree of closeness of the friendship is important. Everyone needs a group of friends who may not always agree with them but who accept them. They are like family yet are peers. This is true for all age groups, and especially for adolescents. Families are our best sounding board, but the family may be too sympathetic or too critical. A group outside family is different in important ways. We all need a group of accepting peers to help us sort out our triumphs and our defeats.

Social organizations can serve this function. At the college level, the larger circle may be the dormitory, sorority, or other fraternal organization. Bridge clubs, church circles, golf buddies, fraternal orders, and other social groups can serve this purpose for adults.

Giving of yourself is a certain way to relieve feelings of loneliness. Through selfless giving—giving without expecting anything in return—our own loneliness is diminished. When coping with loneliness, it is better to give than to receive. As long as our concern is only for self, we continue to feel isolated and lonely. A society that promotes self-indulgence with TV ads that say, "It may cost a lot, but I am worth it" promotes loneliness. Give of yourself, and your reward will be a loss: a loss of loneliness.

The prescription in capsule form for coping with loneliness is: Admit loneliness, take a good look at yourself, reach out to others, be honest with others, share yourself, don't expect too much, look inward, look to your family, find an outside interest, join an organization, make friends, get a pet, and give of yourself. Any of these suggestions will help you fight loneliness, but remember only you can cure your loneliness.

Dag Hammarskjöld, the second secretary-general of the United Nations, wrote in his book, *Markings*, "What makes loneliness an anguish is not that I have no one to share my burden, but this: I have only my own burden to bear." Hammarskjöld's book was published after his death in 1961 in an airplane crash near Ndola, Northern Rhodesia, while flying there on a peace mission for the United Nations. He also wrote: "Pray that your loneliness may spur you into finding something to live for, great enough to die for."

## Loneliness Quotient

If you took the Loneliness Inventory (Short Form) in chapter 1, you know something about your own loneliness. If you would like to know more about your loneliness and situations when you are lonely or not so lonely, complete the Loneliness Inventory (Long Form) found in the Appendix. After you take the test, follow the instructions for scoring that are also in the Appendix.

# Appendix: The Loneliness Inventory

# The Loneliness Inventory

Check the choice that best illustrates how often each of the statements describes your feelings. **Almost always** represents "I almost always feel this way"; **Often** represents "I often feel this way"; **Sometimes** represents "I sometimes feel this way"; **Rarely** represents "I rarely feel this way"; and **Never** represents "I never feel this way." If the item does not apply to your situation (this is a general loneliness inventory, therefore, some questions may not be appropriate for you), check **Does Not Apply.** Be sure to check only one category for each statement.

**I AM LONELY . . . . .**

1. When I am alone.
☐ Almost Always ☐ Often ☐ Sometimes ☐ Rarely ☐ Never ☐ Does Not Apply

2. When I stay alone at night.
☐ Almost Always ☐ Often ☐ Sometimes ☐ Rarely ☐ Never ☐ Does Not Apply

3. When I am with friends.
☐ Almost Always ☐ Often ☐ Sometimes ☐ Rarely ☐ Never ☐ Does Not Apply

4. When I am with my family.
☐ Almost Always ☐ Often ☐ Sometimes ☐ Rarely ☐ Never ☐ Does Not Apply

5. When I am surrounded by people.
☐ Almost Always ☐ Often ☐ Sometimes ☐ Rarely ☐ Never ☐ Does Not Apply

6. When I am in a new and unfamiliar situation.
☐ Almost Always ☐ Often ☐ Sometimes ☐ Rarely ☐ Never ☐ Does Not Apply

7. When things are not going well.
☐ Almost Always ☐ Often ☐ Sometimes ☐ Rarely ☐ Never ☐ Does Not Apply

8. When I am busy.
☐ Almost Always ☐ Often ☐ Sometimes ☐ Rarely ☐ Never ☐ Does Not Apply

9. When I am unoccupied and don't have anything to do.
☐ Almost Always ☐ Often ☐ Sometimes ☐ Rarely ☐ Never ☐ Does Not Apply

10. When I am doing things I enjoy.
☐ Almost Always ☐ Often ☐ Sometimes ☐ Rarely ☐ Never ☐ Does Not Apply

11. When I am doing things I do not enjoy.
☐ Almost Always ☐ Often ☐ Sometimes ☐ Rarely ☐ Never ☐ Does Not Apply

12. When I am with people who are much older than I.
☐ Almost Always ☐ Often ☐ Sometimes ☐ Rarely ☐ Never ☐ Does Not Apply

13. When I am with people who are much younger than I.
☐ Almost Always ☐ Often ☐ Sometimes ☐ Rarely ☐ Never ☐ Does Not Apply

14. When I am with children.
☐ Almost Always ☐ Often ☐ Sometimes ☐ Rarely ☐ Never ☐ Does Not Apply

15. When I am alone for long periods of time.
☐ Almost Always ☐ Often ☐ Sometimes ☐ Rarely ☐ Never ☐ Does Not Apply

16. When I am with children for long periods of time.
☐ Almost Always ☐ Often ☐ Sometimes ☐ Rarely ☐ Never ☐ Does Not Apply

17. When I am confined to home for long periods of time.
☐ Almost Always ☐ Often ☐ Sometimes ☐ Rarely ☐ Never ☐ Does Not Apply

18. When I am without transportation for a long period of time.
☐ Almost Always ☐ Often ☐ Sometimes ☐ Rarely ☐ Never ☐ Does Not Apply

19. When finances are not available to participate in activities.
☐ Almost Always ☐ Often ☐ Sometimes ☐ Rarely ☐ Never ☐ Does Not Apply

20. When I move from one home to another.
☐ Almost Always ☐ Often ☐ Sometimes ☐ Rarely ☐ Never ☐ Does Not Apply

21. When I don't hear from friends.
☐ Almost Always ☐ Often ☐ Sometimes ☐ Rarely ☐ Never ☐ Does Not Apply

22. When I don't hear from relatives.
☐ Almost Always ☐ Often ☐ Sometimes ☐ Rarely ☐ Never ☐ Does Not Apply

23. When I am separated from people.
☐ Almost Always ☐ Often ☐ Sometimes ☐ Rarely ☐ Never ☐ Does Not Apply

24. When the house is quiet.
☐ Almost Always ☐ Often ☐ Sometimes ☐ Rarely ☐ Never ☐ Does Not Apply

25. After a quarrel (argument, disagreement) with someone.
☐ Almost Always ☐ Often ☐ Sometimes ☐ Rarely ☐ Never ☐ Does Not Apply

26. When I attend a funeral.
☐ Almost Always ☐ Often ☐ Sometimes ☐ Rarely ☐ Never ☐ Does Not Apply

27. When there is no one to talk to.
☐ Almost Always ☐ Often ☐ Sometimes ☐ Rarely ☐ Never ☐ Does Not Apply

28. When I am tired or fatigued.
☐ Almost Always ☐ Often ☐ Sometimes ☐ Rarely ☐ Never ☐ Does Not Apply

29. After a festive occasion is over.
☐ Almost Always ☐ Often ☐ Sometimes ☐ Rarely ☐ Never ☐ Does Not Apply

30. When I feel people take advantage of me.
☐ Almost Always ☐ Often ☐ Sometimes ☐ Rarely ☐ Never ☐ Does Not Apply

31. When I feel sorry for myself.
☐ Almost Always ☐ Often ☐ Sometimes ☐ Rarely ☐ Never ☐ Does Not Apply

32. When I don't feel appreciated by others.
☐ Almost Always ☐ Often ☐ Sometimes ☐ Rarely ☐ Never ☐ Does Not Apply

33. When I must do daily tasks and have no one with whom to share the responsibility.
☐ Almost Always ☐ Often ☐ Sometimes ☐ Rarely ☐ Never ☐ Does Not Apply

34. When I can't seem to develop friendships.
☐ Almost Always ☐ Often ☐ Sometimes ☐ Rarely ☐ Never ☐ Does Not Apply

35. When I long to see a familiar face.
☐ Almost Always ☐ Often ☐ Sometimes ☐ Rarely ☐ Never ☐ Does Not Apply

36. When I feel as though I am in a world all by myself.
☐ Almost Always ☐ Often ☐ Sometimes ☐ Rarely ☐ Never ☐ Does Not Apply

37. When my relationships with people lack meaning, warmth, and satisfaction.
☐ Almost Always ☐ Often ☐ Sometimes ☐ Rarely ☐ Never ☐ Does Not Apply

38. When it seems the world goes on its merry way, but I'm not part of it.
☐ Almost Always ☐ Often ☐ Sometimes ☐ Rarely ☐ Never ☐ Does Not Apply

39. When I must care for a sick child or person for a long period of time.
☐ Almost Always ☐ Often ☐ Sometimes ☐ Rarely ☐ Never ☐ Does Not Apply

40. When I must make a decision but have no one with whom to share this responsibility.
☐ Almost Always ☐ Often ☐ Sometimes ☐ Rarely ☐ Never ☐ Does Not Apply

41. When I feel left out or rejected by others.
☐ Almost Always ☐ Often ☐ Sometimes ☐ Rarely ☐ Never ☐ Does Not Apply

42. When I feel left out or rejected by my family.
☐ Almost Always ☐ Often ☐ Sometimes ☐ Rarely ☐ Never ☐ Does Not Apply

43. When I see others doing something I wish I could do.
☐ Almost Always ☐ Often ☐ Sometimes ☐ Rarely ☐ Never ☐ Does Not Apply

44. When I see others doing something I wish I had the ability to do.
☐ Almost Always ☐ Often ☐ Sometimes ☐ Rarely ☐ Never ☐ Does Not Apply

45. When no one understands me.
☐ Almost Always ☐ Often ☐ Sometimes ☐ Rarely ☐ Never ☐ Does Not Apply

46. When I am unsure of myself.
☐ Almost Always ☐ Often ☐ Sometimes ☐ Rarely ☐ Never ☐ Does Not Apply

47. When I am with a stranger.
☐ Almost Always ☐ Often ☐ Sometimes ☐ Rarely ☐ Never ☐ Does Not Apply

48. When I am thinking about the past.
☐ Almost Always ☐ Often ☐ Sometimes ☐ Rarely ☐ Never ☐ Does Not Apply

49. When I am thinking about someone special who is no longer alive.
☐ Almost Always ☐ Often ☐ Sometimes ☐ Rarely ☐ Never ☐ Does Not Apply

50. When I think about death—my own mortality.
☐ Almost Always ☐ Often ☐ Sometimes ☐ Rarely ☐ Never ☐ Does Not Apply

51. When I must make a decision by myself.
☐ Almost Always ☐ Often ☐ Sometimes ☐ Rarely ☐ Never ☐ Does Not Apply

52. When no one will listen to my problems.
☐ Almost Always ☐ Often ☐ Sometimes ☐ Rarely ☐ Never ☐ Does Not Apply

53. When I can't do things for others.
☐ Almost Always ☐ Often ☐ Sometimes ☐ Rarely ☐ Never ☐ Does Not Apply

54. When I am out of place at a particular time or event.
☐ Almost Always ☐ Often ☐ Sometimes ☐ Rarely ☐ Never ☐ Does Not Apply

55. When I don't have the facilities to entertain my friends.
☐ Almost Always ☐ Often ☐ Sometimes ☐ Rarely ☐ Never ☐ Does Not Apply

56. When I don't have room to have overnight guests.
☐ Almost Always ☐ Often ☐ Sometimes ☐ Rarely ☐ Never ☐ Does Not Apply

57. When I am only temporarily located in a community or neighborhood.
☐ Almost Always ☐ Often ☐ Sometimes ☐ Rarely ☐ Never ☐ Does Not Apply

58. When I can't seem to make myself join in group activities.
☐ Almost Always ☐ Often ☐ Sometimes ☐ Rarely ☐ Never ☐ Does Not Apply

59. When almost all the conversations with friends is either gossip or trivia.
☐ Almost Always ☐ Often ☐ Sometimes ☐ Rarely ☐ Never ☐ Does Not Apply

60. When I think about life and how desperately alone each individual really is.
☐ Almost Always ☐ Often ☐ Sometimes ☐ Rarely ☐ Never ☐ Does Not Apply

61. When I want to join in an activity but find circumstances prevent it.
☐ Almost Always ☐ Often ☐ Sometimes ☐ Rarely ☐ Never ☐ Does Not Apply

62. When it seems that God has forsaken me.
☐ Almost Always ☐ Often ☐ Sometimes ☐ Rarely ☐ Never ☐ Does Not Apply

63. When I feel there is no God.
☐ Almost Always ☐ Often ☐ Sometimes ☐ Rarely ☐ Never ☐ Does Not Apply

64. When I don't understand why things have to happen to me.
☐ Almost Always ☐ Often ☐ Sometimes ☐ Rarely ☐ Never ☐ Does Not Apply

65. When I fear people will reject me
☐ Almost Always ☐ Often ☐ Sometimes ☐ Rarely ☐ Never ☐ Does Not Apply

66. When my (child-children) are gone for long periods of time.
☐ Almost Always ☐ Often ☐ Sometimes ☐ Rarely ☐ Never ☐ Does Not Apply

67. When my (child-children) are gone for short periods of time.
☐ Almost Always ☐ Often ☐ Sometimes ☐ Rarely ☐ Never ☐ Does Not Apply

68. After being with old friends.
☐ Almost Always ☐ Often ☐ Sometimes ☐ Rarely ☐ Never ☐ Does Not Apply

69. On my birthday.
☐ Almost Always ☐ Often ☐ Sometimes ☐ Rarely ☐ Never ☐ Does Not Apply

70. When I spend Christmas or other holidays alone.
☐ Almost Always ☐ Often ☐ Sometimes ☐ Rarely ☐ Never ☐ Does Not Apply

71. When I see others "happily" married.
☐ Almost Always ☐ Often ☐ Sometimes ☐ Rarely ☐ Never ☐ Does Not Apply

72. When I am bored.
☐ Almost Always ☐ Often ☐ Sometimes ☐ Rarely ☐ Never ☐ Does Not Apply

73. When I am depressed.
☐ Almost Always ☐ Often ☐ Sometimes ☐ Rarely ☐ Never ☐ Does Not Apply

74. When I think about my family.
☐ Almost Always ☐ Often ☐ Sometimes ☐ Rarely ☐ Never ☐ Does Not Apply

75. When a holiday season such as Christmas is over.
☐ Almost Always ☐ Often ☐ Sometimes ☐ Rarely ☐ Never ☐ Does Not Apply

## Scoring Procedures

Add all your "Almost Always" responses and multiple by 4.

Number of "Almost Always" ——— × 4 = ———.

Add all your "Often" responses and multiply by 3.

Number of "Often" ——— × 3 = ———.

Add all your "Sometimes" responses and multiply by 2.

Number of "Sometimes" ——— × 2 = ———.

Add all your "Rarely" responses and multiply by 1.

Number of "Rarely" ——— × 1 = ———.

Add all your "Never" responses and multiply by 0.

Number of "Never" ——— × 0 = ———.

Add all your scores for each response (total score) = ———.

Divide your total score by 75.

Total Score ——— ÷ 75 = ———.

This is your loneliness score. ———.

# References

## References

Bachman, G. 1970. *Youth in Transition*. Vol. 2. Institute for Social Research, University of Michigan. Ann Arbor: Braun-Brumfield.

Bauermeister, M.L. 1978. "Loneliness among Single Adolescent Mothers." Master's thesis, University of Nebraska–Lincoln.

Butler, R.N. 1975. *Why Survive? Being Old in America*. New York: Harper & Row.

Cutrona, C.E., and Peplau, L.A. 1979. "Loneliness and the Process of Social Adjustment." Paper presented at the annual meeting of American Psychological Association, Toronto, September.

Donlan, J.T. 1978, "Loneliness among Hemophiliacs." Master's thesis, University of Nebraska–Lincoln.

Forum. 1979. *National Action Form for Older Women* (Fall): 2.

Fromm, E. 1956. *The Art of Loving*. New York: Harper & Row.

Gladbach, D.A. 1976. "Loneliness among Selected Adolescents with Physical Impairments." Master's thesis, University of Nebraska–Lincoln.

Graham B. 1969. "Loneliness: How Can It Be Cured?" *Readers Digest*, 135–138.

Hammarskjöld, Dag. 1973. *Markings*. New York: Alfred A. Knopf.

Hornung, K.L. 1980. "Loneliness among Older Urban Widows." Ph.D. dissertation, University of Nebraska–Lincoln.

Joern, J.B. 1973. "Loneliness among Low-Income Single Parent Mothers." Master's thesis, University of Nebraska–Lincoln.

Lair, J. 1972. *I Aint Much Baby, Baby—But I'm All I've Got.* New York, Fawcett Crest.

Medora, N.P. 1983. "Variables Affecting Loneliness among Individuals Undergoing Treatment in Alcohol Rehabilitation Centers." Ph.D. dissertation, University of Nebraska–Lincoln.

Medora, N.P., and Woodward J.C. 1986. "Loneliness among Adolescent College Students at a Midwestern University." *Adolescence* 21(82) 391–402.

Moustakas, C.E. 1961. *Loneliness.* Englewood Cliffs, N.J.: Prentice-Hall.

Otto, B.W. 1973. "Loneliness among Freshman and Senior Class Students in Selected Rural Nebraska Public High Schools." Master's thesis, University of Nebraska–Lincoln.

Russell, D., Peplau, A., and Cutrona, C.E. 1980. "The Revised UCLA Loneliness Scale: Concurrent and Discriminant Validity Evidence." *Journal of Personality and Social Psychology* 39(3): 472–80.

Schachter, S. 1959. *The Psychology of Affiliation.* Stanford, Calif.: Stanford University Press.

Seevers, S.K. 1972. "Loneliness and the College Student." Master's thesis, University of Nebraska–Lincoln.

Swanson, C.K. 1971. "Loneliness as Related to the Never-Married Person." Master's thesis, University of Nebraska–Lincoln.

Tournier, P. 1961 *Escape from Loneliness.* Philadelphia: Westminster Press.

Travis, P. 1975. "Loneliness among Preschool Children." Master's thesis, University of Nebraska–Lincoln.

Visser, M.J. 1971. "Loneliness among Housewives." Master's thesis, University of Nebraska–Lincoln.

Weiss, R. 1974. "The Provisions of Social Relationships." In Z. Rubin (ed.), *Doing unto others*. Englewood Cliffs, N.J.: Prentice-Hall.

Woodward, H. 1971. "Loneliness among the Elderly." Master's thesis, University of Nebraska–Lincoln.

Woodward, J.C. 1967. "Loneliness and Solitude: Phenomena, Incidence and Factorial Relationships." Project Number 93-11. Lincoln: University of Nebraska–Lincoln, Agricultural Experiment Station.

———. 1985. "Loneliness and Urban High School Girls." Departmental research report, University of Nebraska–Lincoln.

———. 1987. "Rural Families and Loneliness—Incidence, Extent, Factorial Relationships and Coping Strategies. Project Number 93-20. Lincoln: University of Nebraska–Lincoln, Agricultural Research Division.

Wythers, M. 1974. "Loneliness among Residents in Homes for the Elderly." Master's thesis, University of Nebraska–Lincoln.

Zabel, J.R. 1970. "Loneliness and Divorce." Master's thesis, University of Nebraska–Lincoln.

# Index

# About the Authors

JOHN C. WOODWARD is a professor in the Department of Human Development and the Family, University of Nebraska–Lincoln. He teaches courses in research design and methodology, child development, and marriage and family relations. His research focuses on loneliness and solitude and is supported by the Agricultural Research Division at the University of Nebraska–Lincoln. He is coauthor of *The Amateur Psychologist's Dictionary* (with Robert M. Diamond). His research on loneliness has been reported on extensively.

JANEL QUEEN is assistant director of the Career Planning and Placement Center, University of Nebraska–Lincoln. She was formerly Dr. Woodward's graduate assistant and coauthored three articles for professional journals with him.